Rosina Filippi

Duologues and Scenes from the Novels of Jane Austen

www.elv-verlag.de

Filippi, Rosina

Duologues and Scenes from the Novels of Jane Austen

ISBN: 978-3-86267-252-3

First published in 2011 by Europaeischer Literaturverlag GmbH, Bremen, Germany.

Europäischer Literaturverlag GmbH, Fahrenheitstr. 1, 28359 Bremen (www.elv-verlag.de).

This book is a reproduction of an out of print title and has originally been published by J. M. Dent & Company (London) in 1895. Because no electronic master copies of this title could be obtained, the publisher had to reuse old copies of the text. We therefore apologize for any possible loss in quality.

DUOLOGUES AND SCENES FROM THE NOVELS OF JANE AUSTEN ARRANGED AND ADAPTED FOR DRAWING-ROOM PERFORMANCE

BY ROSINA FILIPPI (Mrs Dowson)

With Illustrations by MISS FLETCHER

LONDON: Published by J. M. DENT and COMPANY at ALDINE HOUSE in Great Eastern Street, E.C.
MDCCCXCV

PREFACE.

IT is an ungrateful task to write a preface, for few people, if any, ever read one.

"The play's the thing," and "a good play needs no epilogue." So should a good book need no preface, and for one that can boast of containing between its two covers seven picked scenes from the pen of one of the most charming writers in the English language—Jane Austen—no introduction whatever is needed. But to ruthlessly tear her from the library shelf and place her in the hands of the amateur actor demands explanation and even apology.

Jane Austen as a novelist has won and maintained a place in the first rank, but as a writer of true comedy she has been too long unrecognised. She is essentially dramatic, and her characters assume shape, form, and colour; her plots are human, her people are alive. No individual in any of her novels degenerates into caricature, yet there is not one but has a touch of the humorous in his or her composition. Her duologues and scenes are complete in themselves, and in them one appreciates the maxim of Alexandre Dumas, who declared that the *only* essentials for a play were "*une passion, deux personages, et un paravent.*"

Keeping, therefore, to this rule, these scenes should be represented with no scenery whatever—(by scenery, I mean stage, proscenium, footlights, and curtain)—but it is essential that the accurate costume of the day should be worn; for though the plot and sentiments thoroughly appeal to the modern mind, the language belongs to a past generation, and an incongruity would arise were it spoken in modern dress. The period represented is from 1792-1807, and a pen and ink sketch of the type of character and style of dress, the work of Miss Margaret Fletcher, accompanies each scene.

In order to make the plots clear and the duologues intelligible to those of the audience who are unacquainted with the novels themselves, a few words in monologue form have sometimes been added to the text—the greatest care being taken, however, to keep as much as possible to the spirit of the original—while for dramatic effect and finish, the time or place of action has often been changed from a garden or street scene to that of an interior, lest the absence of scenery should be felt by actors or audience.

The idea of compiling this small book arose from the dearth of good duologues and one-act plays suitable for amateur performance. The acting rights of the best pieces being reserved, it is difficult for the uninitiated to obtain them; moreover, it is expensive, and so the orange-covered book is sought, and a play neither clever nor interesting selected, simply because it is found to contain the requisite number of characters, and has no elaborate scenery.

How refreshing, then, must these seven

scenes be to both artists and audience—they play themselves — the language, sentiments, and personalities are within the reach of every cultivated amateur; and I am convinced that Jane Austen *as a play-wright* will fascinate her audiences as much as she has her readers *as a novelist*.

ROSINA FILIPPI.

CONTENTS.

I. LITERARY TASTES . . . . *Page* 1
    Duologue between Catherine Morland and Isabella Thorpe (in the Pump Room, Bath)
        "*Northanger Abbey*"

II. THE SETTLEMENT QUESTION . . ,, 15
    Duologue between Mr and Mrs John Dashwood
        "*Sense and Sensibility*"

III. THE READING OF JANE FAIRFAX'S LETTER . . . . . ,, 31
    Duologue between Miss Bates and Emma
        "*Emma*"

IV. A STRAWBERRY PICNIC . . . ,, 51
    Duologue between Mrs Elton and Mr Knightley
        "*Emma*"

CONTENTS.

V. THREE LOVES . . . . . *Page* 65
  Duologues between Emma and Harriet, and
  Emma and Mr Knightley
    "*Emma*"

VI. THE PROPOSAL OF MR COLLINS . ,, 101
  Dialogue between Mrs Bennet, Elizabeth
  Bennet, and Mr Collins
    "*Pride and Prejudice*"

VII. LADY CATHERINE'S VISIT . .. ,, 123
  Duologue between Lady Catherine and
  Elizabeth Bennet
    "*Pride and Prejudice*"

LIST OF ILLUSTRATIONS.

Costumes	*Frontispiece*
Isabella Thorpe and Catherine Morland	Page 3
Mr and Mrs John Dashwood . .	,, 17
Miss Bates and Emma . . .	,, 33
Mrs Elton and Mr Knightley .	,, 53
Emma and Harriet	,, 67
Elizabeth Bennet and Mr Collins .	,, 103
Lady Catherine and Elizabeth Bennet	,, 125

COSTUMES.

LADIES.

THE prevailing materials for the morning dresses of this period were cambrics, India muslins, clear muslins, usually white, and often spotted and sprigged with clear colours. The bodices were usually cut low with short sleeves, the neck being covered with an embroidered habit shirt or chemisette, often cut with very high collars coming up to the ears. The arms were covered with sleeves of rucked muslin or net. The walking dresses were worn to the ankle only, but the more graceful house dress was worn long. "Spencers," or short bodices, with sleeves made of silk or cloth, were often worn over the muslin dress out of doors; these were sometimes buttoned down the centre, sometimes double-breasted, sometimes left open. "Spanish vests," a sort of Spencer, with long-pointed ends in front, were often seen. Shawls, and long scarfs with embroidered ends, were almost invariable accompaniments of out-door dress, and were carried over the arm or worn draped over one shoulder, or round the neck, with long ends hanging in front like a boa. The use of muslins, furs, China silks, sarsnets, satins, etc., indiscriminately, was characteristic of the period. A dress of India muslin and a fur muff and boa was not considered incongruous. Small hats and turban-shaped caps were as much worn as large; ostrich and herons' feathers, satins, velvets, velvet flowers, and even jewels were used for these. Gloves were usually of York tan or French kid, but sometimes were of *net*. Shoes were made of varying materials—coloured kid, often velvet or silk. The colours most in vogue were pinks, lilacs, violets, lavender, pale primrose, pale greens—scarlets often for pelisses—and all clear colours. Browns are described as "cinamon," chocolate, nut, "la boue de Paris," Egyptian brown, etc. All muslin dresses were worn over "slips" of silk or cambric. In making the bodices, it should be borne in mind that of the many ways of cutting them, the least graceful is to have a straight line round the waist. The line should curve upwards from beneath the bosom in front and reach the highest point between the shoulder-blades at the back, as seen in the back view of Emma. A double curve, which rises slightly in front as well, as seen in one of the distant figures in the frontispiece, is very becoming.

GENTLEMEN.

The men's dress of this period had all the variety of a time of transition—cut-away and swallow-tail coats as well as riding coats and surtouts were worn, differing mainly from the garments of to-day in the height of the waist, and often extravagant height of the collar. The waistcoats were high-waisted, of the gayest colours and most varied materials, being ornamented with fantastic buttons. Pantaloons, either buttoned just above the ankle, or tied with a riband, were in almost universal use; these were supplemented out of doors by top-boots or gaiters. The pantaloons were usually of cloth, though occasionally knitted wool was worn. High stocks and frilled shirt-fronts were usual, but would not have reached an eccentric pitch among Miss Austen's quiet country folks. Hats were high-crowned, with curved brims of varying width, and were made of beaver, felt, or straw. Knee-breeches would be worn by the old-fashioned folk, and by clergymen. The colouring being centred in the waistcoat, the rest of the costume, though perhaps slightly gayer than that of the present day, would on the whole be sober in hue.

LITERARY TASTES.

Duologue between Catherine Morland and Isabella Thorpe.

From "Northanger Abbey."

Costumes.

Isabella is wearing a pelisse of lilac-coloured sarsanet, trimmed with white swansdown; a French cambric frock fastened down the front with small round pearl buttons, and with a border of gold-coloured embroidery round the skirt, which is of walking length. The bodice is cut low, a muslin chemisette with high collar and frill being worn to cover the neck.

The hat of straw or white beaver is tied under the chin by a tan-coloured ribbon, which passes over the crown; a tuft of white ostrich feathers on the left side; tan gloves and tan shoes.

Catherine wears a large natural-coloured straw hat, with jonguille green ribbon and white feathers. A dress of cambric muslin spotted with pale yellow flowers, short full sleeves, and a primrose-coloured shawl; white or tan gloves.

Isabella Thorpe and Catherine Morland.

LITERARY TASTES.

Characters.

Isabella Thorpe and Catherine Morland.

N.B.—" The progress of the friendship between Catherine and Isabella was quick as its beginning had been warm; and they passed so rapidly through every gradation of increasing tenderness, that there was shortly no fresh proof of it to be given to their friends or themselves. They called each other by their Christian name, were always arm-in-arm when they walked, pinned up each other's train for the dance, and were not to be divided in the set; and, if a rainy morning deprived them of other enjoyments, they were still resolute in meeting, in defiance of wet and dirt, and shut themselves up to read novels. . . . The following conversation, which took place between the two friends in the

Pump-room one morning, after an acquaintance of eight or nine days, is given as a specimen of their very warm attachment, and of the delicacy, discretion, originality of thought, and literary taste which marked the reasonableness of that attachment."—*Northanger Abbey*, Chap. V. and VI.

Scene—Part of the Pump-room at Bath.

Properties required:—A sofa R.C.; a small table L., with the visitors' book upon it. Door L. A window up R.C. Enter Isabella Thorpe. Having to wait a few moments, she shows every sign of impatience. Enter Catherine Morland.

Isabella (rising suddenly). My dearest creature! what can have made you so late? (*They embrace.*) I have been waiting for you at least this age.

Catherine (surprised). Have you, indeed? I am very sorry for it, but really I thought I was in very good time (*pointing to her watch or a timepiece*); it is but just one. I hope you have not been here long?

Isabella. Oh! these ten ages at least. I am sure I have been here this half-hour; but now, let us sit down and enjoy ourselves. (*They sit on the sofa.*) I have a hundred things to say to you. In the first place, I was so afraid it would rain this morning, just as I wanted to set off: it looked very showery, and that would have thrown me into agonies! Do you know, I saw the prettiest hat you can imagine in a shop window in Milsom Street just now—very like yours, only with coquelicot ribands instead of green; I quite longed for it. But, my dearest Catherine, what have you been doing with yourself this morning? Have you gone on with "Udolpho"?

Catherine. Yes, I have been reading it ever since I awoke, and I am got to the black veil.

Isabella. Are you, indeed? How delightful! Oh! I would not tell you what is behind the black veil for the world! Are you not wild to know?

Catherine. Oh! yes, quite, what can it be? But do not tell me—I would not be told upon any account. I know it must be a skeleton, I am sure it is Laurentina's skeleton. Oh! I am delighted with the book! I should like to spend my whole life in reading it, I assure you; if it had not been to meet you, I would not have come away from it for all the world.

Isabella (embracing Catherine impulsively). Dear creature! how much I am obliged to you; and when you have finished "Udolpho" we will read the Italian together; and I have made out a list of ten or twelve more of the same kind for you.

Catherine. Have you, indeed! How glad I am! What are they all?

Isabella (rising). I will read you their names directly; here they are in my pocket-book—*(takes out a small pocket-book from her reticule and reads)*, "Castle of Walfenbach," "Clermont," "Mysterious Warnings," "Necromancer of the Black Forest," "Midnight Bell," "Orphan of the Rhine," and "Horrid Mysteries"—*(shutting the book).* There! those will last us some time.

Catherine. Yes—pretty well, but are they all horrid? are you sure that they are all horrid?

Isabella (leaning on the sofa, R. end). Yes, quite sure; for a particular friend of mine—a Miss Andrews, a sweet girl, one of the sweetest creatures in the world, has read every one of them. I wish you knew Miss Andrews, you would be delighted with her. She is netting herself the sweetest cloak you can conceive. I think her as beautiful as an angel, and I am so vexed with the men for not admiring her! I scold them all amazingly about it.

Catherine. Scold them! Do you *scold* them for not admiring her?

Isabella. Yes, that I do. There is nothing I would not do for those who are really my friends. I have no notion of loving people by halves; it is not my nature. My attachments are always excessively strong. I told Captain Hunt, at one of our assemblies this winter, that if he was to tease me all night, I would not dance with him unless he would allow Miss Andrews to be as beautiful as an angel. The men think us incapable of real friendship, you know, and I am determined to show them the difference. Now, if I were to hear anybody speak slightingly of you (*embrace*) I should fire up in a moment; but that is not at all likely, for *you* are just the kind of girl to be a great favourite with the men.

Catherine (hanging her head and turning away). Oh! dear! how can you say so?

Isabella. Oh! I know you very well, you have so much animation, which is exactly what Miss Andrews wants; for I must confess there is something amazingly insipid about her. (*Sitting down again.*) Oh! I must tell you, that just after we parted yesterday I saw a young man looking at you so earnestly.

Catherine (turning away still more).

Isabella. I am sure he is in love with you.

Catherine. Oh! Isabella!

Isabella (laughing). It is very true, upon my honour. But I see how it is; you are indifferent to everybody's admiration except that of one gentleman, who shall be nameless. (*Suddenly serious.*) Nay, I cannot blame you, your feelings are easily understood (*rising*); where the heart is really attached, I know very well how little one can be pleased with the attentions of anybody else (*walking to R.*); everything is so insipid, so uninteresting, that does not relate to the beloved object; I can perfectly comprehend your feelings.

Catherine. But you should not persuade me

that I think so very much about Mr Tilney, for perhaps I may never see him again.

Isabella. Not see him again! (*embracing*) my dearest creature, do not talk of it. I am sure you would be miserable if you thought so.

Catherine (*smiling*). No, indeed, I should not. I do not pretend to say that I was not very much pleased with him; but while I have "Udolpho" to read, I feel as if nobody could make me miserable. Oh! the dreadful black veil! My dear Isabella, I am sure there must be Laurentina's skeleton behind it.

Isabella (*taking Catherine's arm and walking up and down*). It is so odd to me that you should never have read "Udolpho" before; but I suppose Mrs Morland objects to novels.

Catherine. No, she does not. She very often reads "Sir Charles Grandison" herself; but new books do not fall in our way.

Isabella. "Sir Charles Grandison"! that is an amazing horrid book, is it not? I remember Miss Andrews could not get through the first volume.

Catherine. It is not like "Udolpho" at all, but yet I think it is very entertaining.

Isabella. Do you, indeed? you surprise me; I thought it had not been readable (*stopping short*). But, my dearest Catherine, have you settled what to wear on your head to-night. I am determined, at all events, to be dressed exactly like you. The men take notice of *that* sometimes, you know.

Catherine (*innocently*). But it does not signify if they do.

Isabella. Signify! Oh! Heavens! I make it a rule never to mind what they say. They are very often amazingly impertinent if you do not treat them with spirit, and make them keep their distance.

Catherine. Are they? Well, I never observed *that.* They always behave very well to me.

Isabella. Oh! They give themselves such airs. They are the most conceited creatures in the world, and think themselves of so much importance. By the bye, though I have thought of it a hundred times, I have always forgot to ask you what is your favourite complexion in a man. Do you like them best dark or fair?

Catherine. I hardly know. I never much

thought about it. Something between both, I think; brown — not fair and not very dark.

Isabella. Very well, Catherine. That is exactly he. I have not forgot your description of Mr Tilney—"A brown skin, with dark eyes and rather dark hair." Well, my taste is different; I prefer light eyes; and as to complexion—do you know—I like a sallow better than any other. But you must not betray me, if you should ever meet with one of your acquaintance answering that description.

Catherine (impulsively). Betray you! what do you mean?

Isabella. Nay, do not distress me—I believe I have said too much already. Pray, let us drop the subject.

Catherine. My dearest Isabella, certainly, if you wish it. (*Aside as Isabella walks towards the door.*) I wonder if it *is* Laurentina's skeleton. Oh! it must be Laurentina's skeleton.

Isabella (*coming suddenly back to Catherine, but looking over her shoulder towards the door*). For Heaven's sake let us move away from this end of the room. Do you know, there are two odious young men who have been staring at me this half hour? They really put me quite out of countenance. Let us go and look at the arrivals in the visiting book. They will hardly follow us there. (*They walk to the book. While Isabella examines the book, Catherine watches the proceedings off L. door.*) They are not coming this way, are they? I hope they are not so impertinent as to follow us. Pray let me know if they are coming. I am determined I will not look up.

Catherine (*at door, with unaffected pleasure*). You need no longer be uneasy; the gentlemen have just left the Pump-room.

Isabella (*turning hastily round*). And which way are they gone? One of them was a very good-looking young man.

Catherine (*going to the window*). They are going towards the Churchyard.

Isabella (*hastily*). Well, I am amazingly glad I have got rid of them; and now, what say you to going to Edgar's Buildings with me and looking at my new hat? You said you should like to see it.

Catherine. With pleasure—only—perhaps we may overtake the two young men.

Isabella. Oh! never mind that. If we make haste, we shall pass by them presently, and I am dying to show you my hat (*taking Catherine's hand and drawing her towards the door.*)

Catherine (*holding back*). But if we only wait a few minutes there will be no danger of our seeing them at all.

Isabella (*with great dignity, still holding Catherine's hand*). I shall not pay them any such compliment, I assure you. I have no notion of treating men with such respect. *That* is the way to spoil them. Come—and see my new hat. (*Exeunt Catherine and Isabella, hurriedly, by the door.*)

Curtain.

THE SETTLEMENT QUESTION.

DUOLOGUE BETWEEN MR AND MRS JOHN DASHWOOD.

From " Sense and Sensibility," Vol. I., chap. II.

Costumes.

Mrs D. Black dress with a Spanish vest trimmed with narrow black velvet; pointed ends in front, finished with black tassels. Skirt trimmed with black ermine velvet to match white ermine opera tippet.

Mr D. In grey and black.

Mr and Mrs John Dashwood.

THE SETTLEMENT QUESTION.

(A Conversation.)

Characters.

Mr and Mrs John Dashwood.

Scene—*The morning room at Norlands. It is a comfortably furnished room.*

Properties required:—*Door R. Window C. Tables R. and L. Chairs on either side. Books and a work basket with household mending in it.*

N.B.—" He (Mr John Dashwood) was not an ill-disposed young man, unless to be rather cold-hearted, and rather selfish is to be ill-disposed; but he was, in general, well respected, for he conducted himself with propriety in the discharge of his ordinary duties. Had he married a more amiable woman, he might have been still more respectable than he was; he might even have been made amiable himself, for he was very young when he married, and very fond of his wife. But Mrs Dashwood was a strong caricature of himself; more narrow-minded and selfish."—*Sense and Sensibility*, Chap. I.

Enter Mrs John Dashwood, Door R. She is in mourning.

Mrs D. (*going to the window and arranging the curtains.*) A comfortably appointed house—a little shabby, perhaps—but with judicious alterations here and there, I do not doubt of making it very fit and habitable for Mr Dashwood and myself. (*Sitting to her work.*) Yet I wish my father-in-law had not died here, and thus put me to the inconvenience of offering a home to his widow and three daughters till they have found a suitable house of their own. I think I made it palpably clear to them that their stay could only be considered in the light of a visit, by arriving with dear little Harry and our attendants as soon as the funeral was over.

The house was my husband's from the moment of his father's decease, and no one could dispute my right to come. But such is the indelicacy and selfishness of our mother-in-law, that unless my husband finds her a home elsewhere, she and her daughters will consider they may remain here for ever. I hope Mr Dashwood will see that they are soon settled, and then I can take up my proper position at Norlands.

Enter Mr John Dashwood. He, too, is in mourning.

Mr D. My dear, if you are at leisure I should like to speak with you about the promise I made to my late lamented father upon his death-bed respecting the future of my step-mother and three sisters.

Mrs D. The very thing I was thinking of myself.

Mr D. I am happy to see we are in such accord. The case is this. My present income, which is not inconsiderable, will now be increased by four thousand a-year, and the prospect has determined me to behave with generosity. I therefore propose to give them three thousand pounds.

Mrs D. (*with horror*). Three thousand pounds!

Mr D. Yes. It will be liberal and handsome. I can spare so considerable a sum with little inconvenience, and it would be enough to make them completely easy.

Mrs D. But, my dear Mr Dashwood, pray consider. To take three thousand pounds from the fortune of our dear little boy would be impoverishing him to the most dreadful degree. I beg you to think again on the subject. How can you answer it to yourself to rob your child, your only child too, of so large a sum? and what possible claims can the Miss Dashwoods, who are related to you only by half blood, which I consider as no relationship at all, have on your generosity to so large an amount? It is very well known that no affection is ever supposed to exist between the children of any man by different marriages; and why are you to ruin yourself and our poor little Harry, by giving away all your money to your half sisters?

Mr D. It was my father's last request to me, that I should assist his widow and daughters.

Mrs D. He did not know what he was talking of, I dare say. Ten to one but he was light-headed at the time. Had he been in his right senses, he could not have thought of such a thing as begging you to give away half your fortune from your own child.

Mr D. He did not stipulate for any particular sum, my dear Fanny; he only requested me, in general terms, to assist them, and make their situation more comfortable than it was in his power to do. Perhaps it would have been as well if he had left it wholly to myself. He could hardly suppose I should neglect them. But—as he required the promise, I could not do less than give it—at least, I thought so at the time. The promise, therefore, was given, and must be performed. Something must be done for them whenever they leave Norland and settle in a new home.

Mrs D. Well, then, *let* something be done for them; but *that* something need not be three thousand pounds. Consider, that when the money is once parted with, it never can return. Your sisters will marry, and it will be gone for ever,—if, indeed, it could ever be restored to our poor little boy.

Mr D. (*gravely*). Why, to be sure, that would make a difference. The time may come when Harry will regret that so large a sum was parted with. If he should have a numerous family, for instance, it would be a very convenient addition.

Mrs D. To be sure it would.

Mr D. Perhaps, then, it would be better for all parties if the sum were diminished one half. Five hundred pounds would be a prodigious increase to their fortune.

Mrs D. Oh! beyond anything great! What brother on earth would do half so much for his sisters, even if *really* his sisters! And as it is—only half blood! But you have such a generous spirit!

Mr D. I would not wish to do anything mean; one had rather, on such occasions, do too much than too little. No one, at least, can think I have not done enough for them. Even themselves, they can hardly expect more.

Mrs D. There is no knowing what *they* may expect. But we are not to think of their expectations; the question is, what you can afford to do.

Mr D. Certainly; and I think I can afford to give them five hundred pounds a-piece. As it is, without any addition of mine, they will each have above three thousand pounds on their mother's death—a very comfortable fortune for any young woman.

Mrs D. To be sure it is; and, indeed, it strikes me that they can want no addition at all. They will have ten thousand pounds divided amongst them. If they marry they will be sure of doing well, and if they do not, they will live very comfortably together on the interest of ten thousand pounds.

Mr D. That is very true, and, therefore, I do not know whether, upon the whole, it would not be more advisable to do something for their mother while she lives, rather than for them—something of the annuity kind I mean. My sisters would feel the good effects of it as well as herself. A hundred a year would make them all perfectly comfortable.

Mrs D. (*hesitating*). To be sure it is better than parting with fifteen hundred pounds at once;

but then, if Mrs Dashwood should live fifteen years, we shall be completely taken in.

Mr D. Fifteen years! my dear Fanny, her life cannot be worth half that purchase.

Mrs D. Certainly not, but if you observe, people always live for ever when there is any annuity to be paid them; and she is very stout, and healthy, and hardly forty. An annuity is a very serious business; it comes over and over every year, and there is no getting rid of it. You are not aware of what you are doing. I have known a great deal of the trouble of annuities, for my mother was clogged with the payment of three to old superannuated servants by my father's will, and it is amazing how disagreeable she found it. Twice every year these annuities were to be paid; and then there was the trouble of getting it to them: and then one of them was said to have died, and afterwards it turned out to be no such thing. My mother was quite sick of it. Her income was not her own she said, with such perpetual claims upon it; and it was the more unkind in my father, because otherwise, the money would have been entirely at my mother's disposal without any restriction whatever. It has given me such an abhorrence of annuities, that I am sure *I* would not pin myself down to the payment of one for all the world.

Mr D. It is certainly an unpleasant thing to have those kind of yearly drains on one's income. One's fortune, as your mother justly says, is *not* one's own. To be tied down to the regular payment of such a sum, on every rent day, is by no means desirable; it takes away one's independence.

Mrs D. Undoubtedly; and, after all, you have no thanks for it, they think themselves secure; you do no more than what is expected, and it raises no gratitude at all. If I were you, whatever I did should be done at my own discretion entirely. I would not bind myself to allow them anything yearly. It may be very inconvenient some years to spare a hundred, or even fifty, pounds from our own expenses.

Mr D. I believe you are right, my love; it will be better that there should be no annuity in the case. Whatever I may give them occasionally will be of far greater assistance than a yearly allowance, because they would only enlarge their style of living if they felt sure of a larger income, and would not be sixpence the richer for it at the end of the year. It will certainly be much the best way. A present of fifty pounds now and then will prevent their ever being distressed for money, and will, I think, be amply discharging my promise to my father.

Mrs D. To be sure it will. Indeed, to say the truth, I am convinced within myself that your father had no idea of your giving them any money at all. The assistance he thought of, I dare say, was only such as might be reasonably expected of you; for instance, such as looking out for a comfortable small house for them, helping them to move their things, and sending them presents of fish and game, and so forth, whenever they are in season. I'll lay my life that he meant nothing further; indeed, it would be very strange and unreasonable if he did. Do but consider, my dear Mr Dashwood, how excessively comfortable your step-mother and her daughters may live on the interest of seven thousand pounds, besides the thousand pounds belonging to each of the girls, which brings them in fifty pounds a year a-piece, and of course they will pay their mother for their board out of it. Altogether they will have five hundred a year amongst them; and what on earth can four women want for more than that? They will live so cheap! ¡Their housekeeping will be nothing at all. They will have no carriage, no horses, and hardly any servants; they will keep no company, and can have no expenses of any kind! Only conceive how comfortable they will be! Five hundred a year! I am sure I cannot imagine how they will spend half of it; and as for your giving them more, it is quite absurd to think of it. They will be much more able to give *you* something.

Mr D. Upon my word, I believe you are perfectly right. My father certainly could mean nothing more by his request to me than what you say. I clearly understand it now, and I will strictly fulfil my engagement by such acts of assistance and kindness to them as you have described. When my step-mother removes into another house my services shall be readily given to accommodate her as far as I can. Some little present of furniture, too, may be acceptable then.

Mrs D. Certainly; but, however, *one* thing must be considered,—that though the furniture goes with this house, and is therefore our own, your father left *all* the china, linen, and plate to your step-mother. Her house will therefore be almost completely fitted up as soon as she takes it.

Mr D. That is a material consideration, undoubtedly; a valuable legacy, indeed! And some of the plate would have been a very pleasant addition to our own stock here.

Mrs D. Yes, and the set of breakfast china is twice as handsome as ours; a great deal too handsome, in my opinion, for any place *they* can ever afford to live in. But, however, so it is. Your father thought only of *them*, and I must say this, that you owe no particular gratitude to him, nor attention to his wishes; for we very well know, that if he could he would have left almost everything in the world to them.

Mr D. My love, I am convinced of the truth

of what you say. It will not only be absolutely unnecessary, but highly indecorous to do more. (*Looking at his watch.*) Eleven o'clock; the carriage should be here. My step-mother has not been out of doors since my father's funeral, and I ordered the carriage to take her and my sisters for a drive.

Mrs D. (*rising and putting away her work*). My dear Mr Dashwood. No! Here I must be firm. It is quite an unnecessary luxury, which they must sooner or later relinquish; and if they are indulged in carriage exercise now, how can they ever be expected to conform to the new mode of life attendant on their reduced circumstances. It is a cruelty, not a kindness, on your part to suggest such a thing. However, rather than that Wilkins should have troubled to harness the horses in vain, I will take little Harry out with me. The air will do him all the good in the world, and you can easily explain to your mother and sisters that it is incumbent upon me to drive round the estate in order to learn a little of its extent and capacity. You can tell them they shall go out another day.

Mr D. My dear Fanny, you are right, your

judgment of such matters can never be at fault. Perhaps I *was* over-hospitable.

Mrs D. (emphatically). My dear Mr Dashwood, of that there is no doubt.

[*Exeunt Mr and Mrs Dashwood.*

End of Scene.

THE READING OF JANE FAIRFAX'S LETTER.

Duologue between Miss Bates and Emma.

From "Emma," Vol. I., Chap. XIX.

Costumes.

Emma. Long curricle coat of jonquil green china silk, lined with fawn-coloured sarsanet: white cambric dress, the bodice with wrap fronts, crossing on the bosom and fastening at the middle of the back. Opera tippet (boa of white swansdown). A cap of "tiara" form of nut-brown silk, trimmed with pointed green leaves and tied under the chin with nut-brown ribbons; large muff of white swansdown.

Miss Bates. Dress of grey or dark brown silk striped with black; chemisette of thick white muslin; apron of black satin; broad ribbon of myrtle green tied round the head in a bow at the top, a black ostrich tip fastened in the ribbon with an antique pebble brooch; an eyeglass fastened round the neck by a long black ribbon.

Miss Bates and Emma.

THE READING OF JANE FAIRFAX'S LETTER.

Characters.

Miss Bates, Mrs Bates, Emma Woodhouse.

N.B.—" After these came a second set, among the most come-at-able of whom were Mrs and Miss Bates . . . almost always at the service of an invitation from Hartfield, and who were fetched and carried home so often that Mr Woodhouse thought it no hardship for either James or the horses. Had it taken place only once a year it would have been a grievance. *Mrs Bates*, the widow of a former Vicar of Highbury, was a very old lady, almost past everything but tea and quadrille. She lived with her single daughter in a very small way, and was considered with all the regard and respect which a harmless old lady, under such untoward circumstances, can excite. *Her daughter* enjoyed a most uncommon degree of popularity for a woman neither young, handsome, rich, nor married. Miss Bates stood in the very worst predicament in the world for having much of the public favour, and she had no intellectual superiority to make atonement to herself, or frighten those who might hate her, into outward respect. She had never boasted either beauty or cleverness. Her youth had passed without distinction, and her middle life was devoted to the care of a failing mother, and the endeavour to make a small income go as far as possible, and yet she was a happy woman, and a woman whom no one named without good-will. It was her own universal good-will and contented temper which worked such wonders. She loved everybody, was interested in everybody's happiness, quick-sighted to everybody's merits, thought herself a most fortunate creature, and surrounded with blessings

in such an excellent mother, and so many good neighbours and friends, and a home that wanted for nothing. The simplicity and cheerfulness of her nature, her contented and grateful spirit, were a recommendation to everybody, and a mine of felicity to herself. She was a great talker upon little matters, full of trivial communications and harmless gossip. . . . These were the ladies whom *Emma* found herself very frequently able to collect; and happy was she, for her father's sake, in the power; though, as far as she herself was concerned, it was no remedy for the absence of Mrs Weston (her former governess and best friend). The quiet gossipings of such women made her feel that every evening so spent was indeed one of the long evenings she had fearfully anticipated."
—*Emma*, Chap. III.

Scene—Mrs Bates' Parlour.

Properties required:—*One table L.C., with Jane Fairfax's letter on it under reticule; two chairs on either side of the table; another table up R., with a cake upon it, and a knife to cut it; another table up L.; in front of a cheerful fire, "a grandfather's chair" left of the table, ~~with~~ its back turned to the audience, in which Mrs Bates is discovered sitting. In order to bring Mrs Bates on the stage without being seen, a screen must be placed before the chair, and when Mrs Bates is seated so as to be almost completely hidden from the audience during the whole of the scene, Miss Bates must enter, draw back the screen, and say in a loud voice to her mother.*

Miss Bates. So kind of Mrs Cole to call upon us so early in the day, and so interested in Jane's letter. She was indeed, ma'am. How pleased you will be to see dear Jane again. You must not think anything more of her illness. There is nothing to be alarmed at in the least. She says so herself in her letter; you remember, I read it to you—*Jane's* letter. (*Miss Woodhouse's voice heard outside.*)

Emma (*outside*). Are Mrs and Miss Bates within this morning?

Miss Bates. Bless me, here is Miss Woodhouse. (*Runs to door.*) Oh! come up, Miss Woodhouse, pray come up. (*Runs to Mrs Bates.*) Ma'am, ma'am, Miss Woodhouse is so kind as to be calling on us. (*Runs to door.*) Oh, Miss Woodhouse, mind the step—so very treacherous. (*Enter Emma, who curtseys first at the door, then to Mrs Bates.*) And have you walked? All the way? I trust your shoes are not wet or damp. (*Runs back to Mrs Bates after offering chair R. of L.C. table, in which Emma sits.*) Miss Woodhouse has walked, ma'am, *all* the way—so kind. And how is dear Mr Woodhouse? I trust he is well; my mother so enjoyed her evening with him when we were all away at Mrs Weston's, a great deal of chat and backgammon. Tea was made downstairs—biscuits and baked apples; and wine before she came away; amazing luck in some of her throws. Are you seated comfortably? Pray is that chair quite?—yes? Let me offer you some sweet-cake (*runs to table R. and cuts piece of cake*). Mrs *Cole* has just been here; just called in for ten minutes, and was so good as to sit an hour with us. She is but just gone, and *she* took a piece of cake and was so kind as to say she liked it very much; therefore I hope, Miss Woodhouse, you will do me the favour to eat a piece, too. (*Emma takes a piece of cake and eats.*)

Miss Bates (*raising her voice and going to her mother*). Ma'am, Miss Woodhouse has taken a piece of sweet-cake—(*to Emma*). Mrs Cole was so kind as to sit some time with us, talking of my niece Jane; for as soon as she came in, she began inquiring after her—Jane is so very great a favourite there. Whenever she is with us, Mrs Cole does not know how to show her kindness enough, and I must say that Jane deserves it as much as anybody can. And so she began inquiring after her directly, saying—"I know you cannot have heard from Jane lately, because it is not her time for writing." And when I immediately said—"But indeed we have, we had a letter this very morning," I do not know that I ever saw anybody more surprised. "Have you, upon your honour?" said she, "well, that is quite unexpected. Do let me hear what she says."

Emma (politely). Have you heard from Miss Jane Fairfax so lately? I am extremely happy: I hope she is well?

Miss Bates. Thank you. You are so kind! (*hunting about for the letter*). Dear! dear! where can the letter be? I had it but a moment ago.

Emma (aside). How provoking: I thought I had timed my visit so as to escape a letter from Jane Fairfax.

Miss Bates. Ah! here it is. I was sure it could not be far off; but I had put my huswife upon it, you see, without being aware, and so it was quite hid, but I had it in my hand so very lately that I was almost sure it must be on the table. I was reading it to Mrs Cole, and, since she went away, I was reading it again to my mother, for it is such a pleasure to her—a letter from Jane—that she can never hear it often enough, so I knew it could not be far off; and here it is, only just under my huswife. And since you are so kind as to wish to hear what she says; but, first of all, I really must, in justice to Jane, apologise for her writing so short a letter, only two pages, you see, hardly two, and in general she fills the whole paper, and crosses half.

Emma (*aside*). For that at least I am thankful.

Miss Bates. My mother often wonders that I can make it out so well. She often says, when the letter is first opened, "Well, Hetty, now I think you will be put to it to make out all that checker-work," and then I tell her, I am sure she would contrive to make it out herself, if she had nobody to do it for her, every word of it—I am sure she would pore over it till she had made out every word. And indeed, though my mother's eyes are not good as they were, she can see amazingly well still, thank God! with the help of spectacles. It is such a blessing! My mother's are really very good indeed. Jane often says, when she is here, "I am sure, grandmamma, you must have had very strong eyes to see as you do. and so much fine work as you have done too! —I only wish my eyes may last me as well."

Emma. Miss Fairfax writes such an excellent hand—it is in itself like fine embroidery.

Miss Bates. You are extremely kind, you who are such a judge, and write so beautifully yourself. I am sure there is nobody's praise that could give us so much pleasure as Miss Woodhouse's. My mother does not hear; she is a little deaf, you know. I must tell her—(*speaking loudly*) — Ma'am, do you hear what Miss Woodhouse is so obliging to say about Jane's handwriting?

Mrs Bates. Eh?

Miss Bates. Miss Woodhouse says Jane's handwriting is like fine embroidery.

Mrs Bates. What, my dear?

Emma (*aside*). This is very trying.

Miss Bates (*louder*). Miss Woodhouse is so very kind as to say that Jane's handwriting is like fine embroidery.

Mrs Bates. Oh!

Miss Bates (*to Emma*). My mother's deafness is very trifling, you see, just nothing at all. By only raising my voice and saying anything, two or three times over, she is sure to hear; but then she is used to my voice. But it is remarkable that she should always hear Jane better than she does me; Jane speaks so distinct! However, she will not find her grandmamma at all deafer than she was two years ago, which is saying a great deal, at my mother's time of life, and it really is full two years, you know, since she was here. We never were so long without seeing her before, and as I was telling Mrs Cole, we shall hardly know how to make enough of her now.

Emma. Are you expecting Miss Fairfax here soon?

Miss Bates. Oh, yes! next week!

Emma. Indeed! that must be a very great pleasure.

Miss Bates. Thank you. You are very kind. Yes, next week. Everybody is so surprised; and everybody says the same obliging things. I am sure she will be as happy to see her friends at Highbury as they can be to see her. Yes, Friday or Saturday; she cannot say which, because Colonel Campbell will be wanting the carriage himself one of those days. So very good of them to send her the whole way! But they always do, you know. Oh! yes, Friday or Saturday next. That is what she writes about. That is the reason of her writing out of rule, as we call it; for, in the common course, we should not have heard from her before next Tuesday or Wednesday.

Emma. Yes, so I imagined—I was afraid there could be little chance of my hearing anything of Miss Fairfax to-day.

Miss Bates. So obliging of you! No, we should not have heard, if it had not been for this particular circumstance, of her being to come here so soon. My mother is so delighted! for she is to be three months with us at least. Three months, she says so, positively, as I am going to have the pleasure of reading to you. The case is, you see, the Campbells are going to Ireland. Mrs Dixon (Colonel and Mrs Campbell's daughter, to whom Jane was companion before her marriage), has persuaded her father and mother to come over and see her directly. They had not intended to go over till the summer, but she is so impatient to see them again; for till she married, last October, she was never away from them so much as a week, which must make it very strange to be —in different kingdoms, I was going to say, but, however, different countries, and so she wrote a very urgent letter to her mother, or her father—I declare I do not know which it was, but we shall see presently in Jane's letter —wrote in *Mr* Dixon's name as well as her own, to press their coming over directly; and they would give them the meeting in Dublin, and take them back to their country seat, Baly-Craig—a beautiful place, I fancy. Jane has heard a great deal of its beauty—from Mr Dixon, I mean—I do not know that she ever heard about it from anybody else,—but it was very natural, you know, that he should like to speak of his own place while he was paying his addresses,—and as Jane used to be very often walking out with them—for Colonel and Mrs Campbell were very particular about their daughter's not walking out often with *only* Mr Dixon, for which I do not at all blame them: of course she heard everything he might be telling Miss Campbell about his own home in Ireland; and I think she wrote us word that he had shown them some drawings of the place, views that he had taken himself. He is a most amiable, charming young man, I believe. Jane was quite longing to go to Ireland from his account of things.

Emma. You must feel it very fortunate that Miss Fairfax should be allowed to come to you at such a time. Considering the very particular friendship between her and Mrs Dixon, you could hardly have expected her to be excused from accompanying Colonel and Mrs Campbell.

Miss Bates. Very true, very true indeed. The very thing we have always been rather afraid of; for we should not like to have her at such a distance from us, for months together, not able to come if anything was to happen; but you see everything turns out for the best. They want her (Mr and Mrs Dixon) excessively to come over with Colonel and Mrs Campbell, quite depend upon it; nothing can be more kind or pressing than their *joint* invitation, Jane says, as you will hear presently. Mr Dixon does not seem in the least backward in any attention. He is a most charming young man. Ever since the service he rendered Jane at Weymouth, when they were out in that party on the water, and she, by the sudden whirling round of something or other among the sails, would have been dashed into the sea at once, and actually was all but gone, if he had not, with the greatest presence of mind, caught hold of her habit,—I can never think of it without trembling!—but ever since we had the history of that day, I have been so fond of Mr Dixon.

Emma. But, in spite of all her friends' urgencies and her own wish to see Ireland, Miss Fairfax prefers devoting the time to you and Mrs Bates.

Miss Bates. Yes, entirely her own doing, entirely her own choice; and Colonel and Mrs Campbell think she does quite right—just what they should recommend; and, indeed, they particularly *wish* her to try her native air, as she has not been quite so well as usual lately.

Emma. I am concerned to hear of it. I think they judge wisely, but Mrs Dixon must be very much disappointed. Mrs Dixon, I understand, is very charming, but has no remarkable degree of personal beauty,—is not by any means to be compared to Miss Fairfax.

Miss Bates. Oh! Miss Woodhouse, how very kind! how very obliging! I must tell my mother (*turning towards Mrs Bates, who is asleep*). Ma'am, did you hear Miss Woodhouse's amiable compliments (*turning to Emma*). Ah! she is asleep; never mind, I will tell her when you are gone—Oh! no—Certainly not—there is no comparison between them—Miss Campbell always was absolutely plain, but extremely elegant and amiable.

Emma. Yes, that of course.

Miss Bates. Jane caught a bad cold, poor thing! so long ago as the 7th of November (as I am going to read to you), and has never been well since. A long time, is it not, for a cold to hang upon her? She never mentioned it before, because she would not alarm us. Just like her! So considerate! But, however, she is so far from well that her kind friends the Campbells think that she had better come home and try an air that always agrees with her, and they have no doubt that three or four months at Highbury will entirely cure her; and it is certainly a great deal better that she should come here than go to Ireland if she is unwell. Nobody could nurse her as we should do.

Emma. It appears to me the most desirable arrangement in the world.

Miss Bates. And so she is to come to us next Friday or Saturday, and the Campbells leave town on their way to Holyhead the Monday following, as you will find from Jane's letter. So sudden! you may guess, dear Miss Woodhouse, what a flurry it has thrown me in! If it was not for the drawback of her illness—but I am afraid we must expect to see her grown thin and looking very poorly. I must tell you what an unlucky thing happened to me as to that. I always make a point of reading Jane's letters through to myself first before I read them aloud to my mother, you know, for fear of there being anything in them to distress her. Jane desired me to do it, so I always do; and so I began to-day with my usual caution: but no sooner did I come to the mention of her being unwell, than I burst out, quite frightened, with "Bless me! poor Jane is ill"—which my mother, being on the watch, heard distinctly, and was sadly alarmed at. However, when I read on, I found it was not near so bad as I fancied at first;

and I make so light of it now to her, that she does not think much about it: but I cannot imagine how I could be so off my guard! If Jane does not get well soon, we will call in Mr Perry. The expense shall not be thought of; and though he is so liberal and so fond of Jane, that I dare say he would not mean to charge anything for attendance, we would not suffer it to be so, you know. He has a wife and family to maintain, and is not to be *giving* away his time. Well now, I have just given you a hint of what Jane writes about. We will turn to her letter, and I am sure she tells her own story a great deal better than I can tell it for her (*turning to the letter*).

Emma (*rising abruptly*). I am afraid I must be running away. My father will be expecting me. I had no intention, I thought I had no power, of staying more than five minutes when I first entered the house. I merely called, because I would not pass the door without enquiring after Mrs Bates; but I have been so pleasantly detained! And now I must wish you and Mrs Bates good morning. (*Curtsies and exit.*)

Miss Bates (during Miss Woodhouse's speech.) Dear Miss Woodhouse, so soon—must you really go; so kind of you to come. Jane's letter so short, only two pages—will not take one minute to read—pray mind the step outside. Allow me. (*Exeunt Miss Bates and Emma.*)

Mrs Bates coughs and picks up her ball of wool. Re-enter Miss Bates.

Miss Bates. Ma'am, Miss Woodhouse assures me it is quite dry under foot. I am sure you would enjoy a little walk up the road with me (*helping her mother up and leading her out of the room, talking all the time*); and I will tell you what Miss Woodhouse was so obliging as to say about Jane's beauty as we go—though perhaps it is hardly the thing to repeat to everybody. She says that Mrs Dixon (*exeunt Mrs and Miss Bates. Miss Bates' voice fading away little by little outside*) has no remarkable degree of beauty, and is not by any means to be compared with our Jane—so kind of her, is it not? Ma'am, ma'am, mind that step—no, not by any means to be compared with our Jane.

End of Scene.

A STRAWBERRY PICNIC.

DUOLOGUE BETWEEN MRS ELTON AND MR KNIGHTLEY.

From "Emma," Vol. II., Chap. XLII.

Costumes.

Mrs Elton. A dress of dove-coloured sarsanet with a ruche of the same round the bottom of skirt; puffings of cream net round the neck; narrow cherry-coloured ribbon round the bodice and down the front of the skirt; fancy straw hat with cream feathers and cherry-coloured ribbons; pale pink shawl to harmonise with ribbons.

Mr Knightley. Buff-coloured coat, with dark velvet collar, high stock; frilled shirt front; short waistcoat of deep blue; cream-coloured breeches.

Mrs Elton and Mr Knightley.

A STRAWBERRY PICNIC.

Characters.

Mrs Elton and Mr Knightley.

N.B.—" *Mrs Elton* was first seen in church. . . . Emma had feelings, less of curiosity than of pride or propriety, to make her resolve on not being the last to pay her respects. . . . She (Emma) was almost sure that for a young woman, a stranger, a bride, there was too much ease. . . . and a quarter of an hour quite convinced her that Mrs Elton was a vain woman, extremely well satisfied with herself and thinking much of her own importance. . . . Emma was not required, by any subsequent discovery, to retract her ill opinion of Mrs Elton. Her observation had been pretty correct—such as Mrs

Elton appeared to her on this second interview, such she appeared whenever they met again—self-important, presuming, familiar, ignorant, and ill-bred."—*Emma*, Vol. II., Chap. XXXII. "You might not see one in a hundred, with *gentleman* so plainly written as in Mr Knightley." . . . "Mr Knightley's downright, decided, commanding sort of manner, though it suits *him* very well: his figure, and look and situation in life seem to allow it; but if any young man were to set about copying him, he would not be sufferable."—*Emma*, Vol. I., Chap. IV.

Scene—*A parlour in Mrs Weston's house.*

Properties required:—*A small table L.C.; a chair L. of it; a writing table in front of a window up R.; a door R.; other chairs and sofas; a general air of comfort and refinement. Enter Mrs Elton—who soon sits with her back to the door.*

Mrs Elton. Provoking! Everything contrives for my annoyance; first, I agree to meet

Mr Elton here, and Mrs Weston is out, and I am forced to wait alone. Then this exploring party that I had set my heart upon is obliged to be put off through a lame horse, then—— (*enter Mr Knightley*). Ah! you have found me out at last in my seclusion? (*turns and sees Knightley.*) Oh! Knightley, it is *you*. I have been waiting in this room this age for my lord and master, who promised to meet me here and pay his respects to Mrs Weston, and as she was out, I was, of course, forced to wait alone. But now that you are come——

Knightley (*stiffly.*) I gathered from Mrs Weston's excellent maid that she was from home, and merely came in to write a note of importance. I did not know you were here, or should not have intruded myself upon you.

Mrs Elton. Why do you speak of intrusion? I am delighted, and although I cannot approve of a husband keeping his wife waiting at any time, still I must make allowances for *Mr Elton*; for he really is engaged from morning to night—there is no end of people's coming to him on some pretence or other. The magistrates and overseers and churchwardens are always wanting his opinion. They seem not able to do anything without him. "Upon my word, Mr E.," I often say, "rather you than I. I do not know what would become of my crayons and my instrument if I had half so many applicants." Bad enough as it is, for I absolutely neglect them both to an unpardonable degree. But is it not most vexatious, Knightley? and such weather for exploring.

Knightley. Pardon me, I do not quite follow you.

Mrs Elton. Oh! have you not heard of our lame carriage-horse? Everything has been put off,—the exploring party to Box Hill.

Knightley. Oh! yes; very annoying, to be sure; but these things will happen, you know, Mrs Elton.

Mrs Elton. I know; but when the *first* disappointment occurred, through Mr and Mrs Suckling not being able to visit Highbury until the autumn, *I* said, why should we not explore to Box Hill though the Sucklings did *not* come? We could go there *again* in the autumn with *them*. And so, as you know, my suggestion was immediately taken up; and everything was so charmingly arranged—why, I had even settled with Mrs Weston as to pigeon pies and cold lamb, when, all at once, everything is thrown into uncertainty. It may be weeks before the horse is usable, and, therefore, no preparations can be ventured upon. What are we to do? The delays and disappointments are quite odious. The year will wear away at this rate, and nothing done. Before this time last year we had delightful exploring parties from Maple Grove to King's Weston, and—

Knightley (*lightly*). You had better explore to Donwell. That may be done without horses. Come and eat my strawberries. They are ripening fast.

Mrs E. (*impulsively*). Oh! I should like it of all things! Donwell, I know, is famous for its strawberry beds. You may depend upon me; I certainly will come; name your day, and I will come; you will allow me to bring Jane Fairfax.

Knightley. I cannot name a day, till I have spoken to some others whom I would wish to meet you.

Mrs Elton. Oh! leave all that to me, only

give me *carte blanche*—I am lady Patroness, you know—It is *my* party—I will bring friends with me.

Knightley. I hope you will bring Elton, but I will not trouble you to give any other invitations.

Mrs Elton. Oh! now you are looking very sly—but consider—you need not be afraid of delegating power to me. Married women, you know, may be safely authorised. It is *my* party—leave it all to me. *I* will invite your guests.

Knightley. No, Mrs Elton, no. There is but one married woman in the world whom I can ever allow to invite what guests she pleases to Donwell, and that one is—

Mrs Elton (mortified). Mrs Weston, I suppose.

Knightley. No—Mrs Knightley, and till *she* is in being, I will manage such matters myself.

Mrs Elton (satisfied to have no one preferred to herself). Ah! you are an odd creature; you are a humorist, and may say what you like—quite a humorist. Well, I shall bring Jane with me—Jane Fairfax and her aunt—the rest I leave to you,—I have no objections at all to meeting the Hartfield family. Don't scruple—I know you are attached to them.

Knightley. You certainly *will* meet them if I can prevail; and I shall call on Miss Bates on my way home.

Mrs Elton. That is quite unnecessary; I see Jane every day;—but, as you like. It is to be a morning scheme, you know, Knightley; quite a simple thing. I shall wear a large bonnet, and bring one of my little baskets hanging on my arm — here — probably this basket—with pink ribbons. Nothing can be more simple, you see. And Jane will have such another. There is to be no form or parade—a sort of gipsy party. We are to walk about your gardens and gather the strawberries ourselves, or sit under the trees; and whatever else you like to provide, it is to be all out of doors—a table spread in the shade, you know. Everything as natural and simple as possible. Is not that your idea?

Knightley. Not quite. My idea of the simple and the natural will be to have the table spread in the dining-room. The nature and simplicity of gentlemen and ladies with their servants and furniture, I think, is best observed by meals within doors. When you are tired of eating strawberries in the garden, there shall be cold meat in the house.

Mrs Elton. Well, as you please; only don't have a great set-out—by-the-bye, can I or my housekeeper be of any use to you with our opinion? Pray be sincere, Knightley. If you wish me to talk to Mrs Hodges or to inspect anything—

Knightley. I have not the least wish for it, thank you.

Mrs Elton. Well!—but if any difficulties should arise; my housekeeper is extremely clever—

Knightley. I will answer for it, mine thinks herself full as clever, and would spurn anybody's assistance.

Mrs Elton. I wish we had a donkey. The thing would be for us *all* to come on donkeys— Jane, Miss Bates, and me, and my *cara sposo* walking by my side. I really must talk to him about purchasing a donkey. In a country life I conceive it to be a sort of necessary; for, let a woman have ever so many resources, it is not possible for her to be always shut up at home; and very long walks you know — in summer there is dust, and in winter there is dirt—

Knightley. You will not find either between Donwell and Highbury.—Donwell lane is never dusty, and now it is perfectly dry. Come on a donkey, however, if you prefer it — you can borrow Mrs Cole's. I would wish everything to be as much to your taste as possible.

Mrs Elton. That I am sure you would. Indeed, I do you justice, my good friend. Under that peculiar sort of dry, blunt manner, I know you have the warmest heart. As I tell Mr E. —you are a thorough humorist. Yes, believe me, Knightley, I am fully sensible of your attention to me in the whole of this scheme. You have hit upon the very thing to please me.

Knightley. Do not mention it, I pray; but, if you will allow me, I will now write my note to Mrs Weston. It is of importance. (*Bows and goes to writing table.*)

Mrs Elton. Oh! don't mind me. I have a thousand pleasant things to think of now. Oh! by-the-bye, don't forget to include Mr and Mrs Weston in your invitations. Do not leave them out: that would be unpardonably amiss—and Mrs Weston's step-son, Frank Churchill, you must invite *him* (*aside*) All this is really most charming. Wright shall do my hair in the simplest fashion. She shall dress it like a shepherdess of the last century, and my gown shall be all white. I look well in white, at least that foolish Elton has often told me so; besides, it is so rural and simple. Nobody can think less of dress than I do; but upon such an occasion as this, when everybody's eyes will be upon me, and in compliment to Knightley, who is giving this picnic party chiefly to do me honour, I would not wish to be inferior to others.

Knightley (*rising from the writing table*). And now, my letter written, I will bid you good-day, and shall soon hope to settle the day for our strawberry feast.

Mrs Elton. Must you be going, really? I cannot imagine what is become of Mr Elton. He should have been here ages ago. He promised to come to me as soon as he could disengage himself from his appointment at "The Crown." They are all shut up with him at a meeting—a regular meeting, you know

—Weston and Cole are there too; but one is apt to speak only of those who lead, and I fancy Mr E. or yourself have everything your own way here. By-the-bye, Knightley, how is it you are not at the meeting?

Knightley. For the simple reason that the meeting you speak of is not until to-morrow.

Mrs Elton. Ah! surely you are mistaken—the meeting is certainly to-day. I do believe this is the most troublesome parish that ever was. We never heard of such things at Maple Grove. Mr E. was certainly under the impression the meeting was to-day, and depend upon it, he was so vexed at finding out his mistake, that he has forgotten entirely his appointment with me here, and my conjugal obedience is merely time and patience thrown away. How provoking! Knightley, you must offer me your arm and escort me some little way; as far as Miss Bates, and there we can settle the precise day our charming exploring party to Donwell shall take place.

Knightley (offering his arm.) With pleasure. I will ask Miss Bates if she and Miss Fairfax will be of the party, but the day must be fixed for the convenience of Mr Woodhouse, whom I am most anxious to receive at my house.

Mrs Elton. Oh! Out of the question. Mr Woodhouse is far too great an invalid. You will not prevail upon him to come at all.

Knightley. I still hope to do so, with his daughter's assistance. *(Exeunt Mr Knightley and Mrs Elton.)*

Mrs Elton (outside). Oh! if Emma Woodhouse wishes it, poor Mr Woodhouse will *have* to come.

End of Scene.

THREE LOVES.

From "Emma."

Costumes.

Emma. Short dress of muslin, sprigged with a blue flower, trimmed with sapphire blue velvet, under sleeves of ruched net, sapphire velvet in the hair.

Harriet. Black silk pelerine, with long ends; white cambric dress; bonnet of white sarsnet, tied with pale rose-coloured ribbons; coral necklace.

Mr Knightley. Buff-coloured coat, with dark velvet collar, high stock; frilled shirt front; short waistcoat of deep blue; cream-coloured breeches.

Emma and Harriet.

THREE LOVES.

Characters.

Emma Woodhouse, Harriet Smith, Mr Knightley.

N.B.—" *Emma Woodhouse,* handsome, clever and rich, with a comfortable home and happy disposition, seemed to unite some of the best blessings of existence, and had lived nearly twenty-one years in the world with very little to distress or vex her. She was the youngest of the two daughters of a most affectionate, indulgent father; and had, in consequence of her sister's (Isabella) marriage, been mistress of his house from a very early period.

The real evils, indeed, of Emma's situation were the power of having rather too much her own way, and a disposition to think a little too well of herself."—*Emma,* Chap. I.

"*Mr Knightley*, a sensible man about seven or eight-and-thirty, was not only a very old and intimate friend of the family, but particularly connected with it as the elder brother of Isabella's husband. He lived about a mile from Hartfield, was a frequent visitor, and always welcome. . . . Mr Knightley had a cheerful manner, which always did him (Mr Woodhouse) good. . . . Mr Knightley, in fact, was one of the few people who could see faults in Emma Woodhouse, and the only one who ever told her of them."—*Emma*, Chap. I.

"*Harriet Smith* was the natural daughter of somebody. Somebody had placed her several years back at Mrs Goddard's school, and somebody had lately raised her from the condition of scholar to that of parlour boarder. This was all that was generally known of her history. . . . She was a very pretty girl, and her beauty happened to be of a sort which Emma particularly admired. . . . She was short, plump, and fair, with a fine bloom, blue eyes, light hair, regular features, and a look of great sweetness. . . . She (Emma) was not struck by anything remarkably clever in Miss Smith's conversation, but she found her altogether engaging—not inconveniently shy, nor unwilling to talk—and yet so far from pushing, showing so proper and becoming a deference, seeming so pleasantly grateful for being admitted to Hartfield, and so artlessly impressed by the appearance of everything in so superior a style to what she had been used to, that she must have good sense and deserve encouragement. Encouragement should be given. . . . *She* would notice her. She would improve her . . . and introduce her into good society; she would form her opinions and manners. . . . As a walking companion, Emma had very early foreseen how useful she might find her . . . and a Harriet Smith, therefore, one whom she could summon at any time to a walk, would be a valuable addition to her privileges. But in every respect, as she saw more of her, she approved her, and was confirmed in all her kind designs."—*Emma*, Chaps. III. and IV.

Scene—The morning-room at Hartfield. It is comfortably furnished. No special properties are required except a centre table with two chairs on either side of it; a work frame near one of the chairs, a window at the back, and a fireplace with a lighted fire. Enter Emma, with an open letter in her hand.

Emma. I can scarcely believe it. Jane Fairfax engaged to Frank Churchill! Engaged to her all the winter—secretly engaged before either of them came to Highbury. And I have encouraged my poor friend, Harriet Smith, to think well of him, so she will be a second time the dupe of my misconceptions and flattery. It seems like a fatality. No sooner do I conceive the idea of arranging a suitable marriage for her, than the man whom I choose deliberately engages himself to another. I ought to have felt only too thankful to have her forget the insufferable

Mr Elton so soon after his marriage, instead of trying to rouse her affections for Frank Churchill. But what right had he to come among us with affection and faith engaged, and with manners so very *disengaged?* How could he tell that he might not be making *me* in love with him? I cannot deny, indeed, that there was a time, in the early period of our acquaintance, when I was very much pleased with his attentions, when I was very much disposed to be attached to him—nay, was attached—and how it came to cease is perhaps the wonder.

Harriet (outside). Miss Woodhouse, are you within, and will you see me?

Emma. Harriet! (*folding the letter hastily and putting it away*). Yes, yes, pray come in. (*Enter Harriet, who curtseys at the door.*) You know I am always glad to see *you*, Harriet. (*Aside.*) I wonder if she has heard the news. She looks dejected.

Harriet (with a small parcel in her hand). Miss Woodhouse, dear Miss Woodhouse, you are always good to me. A great deal too good—

but if you are at leisure, I have something that I should like to tell you; a sort of confession to make, and then, you know, it will be over.

Emma (*sighs, aside*). Poor Harriet.

Harriet. It is my duty, and I am sure it is my wish, to have no reserves with you on this subject. As I am, happily, quite an altered creature in *one respect*, it is very fit that you should have the satisfaction of knowing it. I do not want to say more than is necessary. I am too much ashamed of having given way as I have done, and I daresay you understand me.

Emma. I think I do, my poor Harriet—I hope I do; but it is all my fault—all my fault.

Harriet. Oh! Miss Woodhouse, do not say such a thing! How could I so long a time be fancying myself— It seems like madness, I can see nothing at all extraordinary in him now.

Emma (*aside*). To whom is she alluding— Mr Elton or Frank Churchill? One never can tell.

Harriet. I do not care whether I meet him or not, except that of the two I had rather *not* see him; and, indeed, I would go any distance round to avoid him. But I do not envy *Mrs Elton* in the least.

Emma (aside). Ah! it's Mr *Elton*, not Frank Churchill.

Harriet. She is very charming, I dare say, and all that, but I think her very ill-tempered and disagreeable. However, I assure you, Miss Woodhouse, I wish her no evil. No; let them be ever so happy together, it will not give me another moment's pang; and, to convince you that I have been speaking truth, I am now going to destroy—what I ought to have destroyed long ago—what I ought never to have kept: I know that very well—However, now I will destroy it all; and it is my particular wish to do it in your presence, that you may see how rational I am grown (*sighs*). Cannot you guess what this parcel holds?

Emma. Not the least in the world. Did he ever give you anything?

Harriet. No, I cannot call them *gifts;* but they are things that I have valued very much (*holding out the parcel to Emma*).

Emma (taking it and reading). "Most precious

treasures." Harriet, are you sure you would wish me to see these treasures?

Harriet. Yes, please, dear Miss Woodhouse.

Emma (*undoing the parcel, which is wrapped up in several pieces of paper and lined with cotton wool*). A piece of court plaister!!!

Harriet. Now, you *must* recollect.

Emma. No, indeed, I do not.

Harriet. Dear me! I should not have thought it possible you could forget what passed in this very room about court plaister, one of the very last times we ever met in it. It was a very few days before I had my sore throat—I think the very evening before. Do not you remember his cutting his finger with your new penknife, and your recommending court plaister? But, as you had none about you, and knew I had, you desired me to supply him. So I took mine out and cut him a piece, but in my agitation I cut it a great deal too large, and he had to make it smaller, and kept playing some time with what was left before he gave it back to me. And so then, in my nonsense, I could not help making a treasure of it; so I put it by, never to be used, and looked at it now and then as a great treat.

Emma (*putting her hands before her face*). My dearest Harriet! you make me more ashamed of myself than I can bear. Remember it? Aye, I remember it all now; all except your saving this relic; I knew nothing of that till this moment; but the cutting the finger, and my recommending court plaister and saying I had none about me—Oh! my sins! my sins!—And I had plenty all the while in my pocket! One of my senseless tricks! I deserve to be under a continual blush all the rest of my life.—Well (*sitting down*), go on, what else?

Harriet. And had you really some at hand yourself? I am sure I never suspected it. You did it so naturally.

Emma. And so you actually put this piece of court plaister by for his sake. (*Aside*), Lord bless me! when should I ever have thought of putting by in cotton a piece of court plaister that anybody had been fingering. I shall never be equal to this.

Harriet. There is something still more valuable—I mean that *has been* more valuable because it is what did really once belong to him, which the court plaister never did? It is in the same box wrapped up in another piece of silver paper.

Emma (*unfolding a very small roll*). I am quite anxious to see this superior treasure, Harriet. What is it?—The end of an old pencil! the part without any lead!! What is this, Harriet?

Harriet. That was really his. Do not you remember one morning?—No, I daresay you do not—but one morning—I forget exactly the day, but perhaps it was the Wednesday or Tuesday before *that evening*, he wanted to make a memorandum in his pocket-book; it was about spruce beer. Mr Knightley (*hanging her head*) had been telling him something about brewing spruce beer, and he wanted to put it down; but when he took out his pencil, there was so little lead that he soon cut it all away and it would not do, so you lent him another, and this was left upon the table as good for nothing. But I kept my eye upon it, and as soon as I dared, caught it up, and never parted with it again from that moment.

Emma. I do remember it. I perfectly remember it—talking of spruce beer. Oh! yes, Mr Knightley and I both saying we liked it, and Mr Elton's seeming resolved to learn to like it too. I perfectly remember it—Stop; Mr Knightley was standing just here, was not he? I have an idea he was standing just here.

Harriet (confused). I do not know. I cannot recollect. It is very odd—but I cannot recollect where Mr Knightley was standing. Mr *Elton* was sitting here, I remember, much about where I am.

Emma. Well, go on.

Harriet. Oh! that is all. I have nothing more to show you, or to say, except that I am now going to throw them both behind the fire, and I wish you to see me do it.

Emma. My poor dear Harriet! and have you actually found happiness in treasuring up these things?

Harriet (sighing). Yes, simpleton as I was!—but I am quite ashamed of it now, and wish I could forget as easily as I can burn them. It was so wrong of me, you know, to keep any remembrance after he was married, and when I had conceived so deep, so reverential a regard for *another*. I knew it was, but I had not resolution enough to part with them.

Emma. But, Harriet, is it necessary to burn the court plaister? I have not a word to say for the bit of old pencil, but the court plaister might be useful.

Harriet. I shall be happier to burn it. It has a disagreeable look to me. I must get rid of *everything*. I must not keep it now. It is not right towards *him* who is so superior in every way, so infinitely superior. (*Emma groans.*) These are no longer treasures. There they go (*throwing them into the fire*), and there is an end, thank Heaven! of Mr Elton. (*Turning cheerfully to Emma.*) Ah! I feel happier now—much happier! But, oh! Miss Woodhouse, is not this the oddest news that ever was?

Emma (*perplexed*). What news do you mean?

Harriet. Why, about Jane Fairfax. Did you ever hear anything so strange? Oh! you need not be afraid of owning it to me, for Mr Weston has told me himself. I met him just now. He told me it was to be a great secret; and therefore I should not think of mentioning it to anybody but you, but he said you knew it.

Emma (still perplexed). What did Mr Weston tell you?

Harriet. Oh! he told me all about it; that Jane Fairfax and Mr Frank Churchill are to be married, and that they have been privately engaged to one another this long while. How very odd.

Emma (staring). You know all about it?

Harriet. Yes! Had you any idea of his being in love with her?—you perhaps might (*hanging her head*)—you who can see into everybody's heart; but nobody else—

Emma. Upon my word, I begin to doubt my having any such talent. Can you seriously ask me, Harriet, whether I imagined him attached to another woman at the very time that I was— tacitly, if not openly—encouraging you to give way to your own feelings? I never had the slightest suspicion, till within the last hour, of Mr Frank Churchill's having the least regard for Jane Fairfax. You may be very sure that, if I had, I should have cautioned you accordingly.

Harriet (in astonishment). Me! why should you caution me? You do not think I care about Mr Frank Churchill?

Emma (laughing uneasily). I am delighted to hear you speak so stoutly on the subject. But you do not mean to deny that there was a time—and not very distant either—when you gave me reason to understand that you did care about him.

Harriet. *Him!*—never, never. Dear Miss Woodhouse, how could you so mistake me? (*turning away distressed.*)

Emma. Harriet, what do you mean? (*A pause.*) Good heaven! what do you mean? Mistake you! am I to suppose—?

Harriet (with her back to Emma). I should not have thought it possible that *you* could have misunderstood me! I know we agreed never to name him — but, considering how infinitely superior he is to everybody else, I should not have thought it possible that I could be supposed to mean any other person. Mr Frank Churchill, indeed! I do not know who would ever look at him in the company of the other. And that *you* should have been so mistaken is amazing.

Emma (collecting herself resolutely). Harriet, let us understand each other now, without the possibility of further mistake. (*With great effort.*) Are you speaking—of Mr Knightley?

Harriet. To be sure I am. I never could have an idea of anybody else—and so I thought you knew. When we talked about him, it was as clear as possible.

Emma (with forced calmness). Not quite, for all that you then said appeared to me to relate to a different person. I could almost assert that you *named* Mr Frank Churchill.

Harriet. Oh! Miss Woodhouse, never— never.

Emma. Well, I am sure the service Mr Frank Churchill had rendered you, in protecting you from the gipsies, was spoken of.

Harriet. Miss Woodhouse! how you do forget!

Emma. My dear Harriet, I perfectly remember the substance of what I said on the occasion. I told you that I did not wonder at your attachment; that, considering the service he had rendered you, it was extremely natural:—and you agreed to it, expressing yourself very warmly as to your sense of that service, and mentioning even what your sensations had been in seeing him come forward to your rescue. The impression of it is strong on my memory.

Harriet. Oh! dear! now I recollect what you mean; but I was thinking of something very different at the time. It was not the gipsies.—It was not Mr Frank Churchill that I meant. No—(*with some elevation*)—I was thinking of a much more precious circumstance —of Mr Knightley's coming and asking me to dance, when Mr Elton would not stand up with me, and when there was no other partner in the room. That was the kind action; that was the noble benevolence and generosity; that was the service which made me begin to feel how superior he was to any other being upon earth.

Emma (*with emotion*). Good God! this has been a most unfortunate—most deplorable mistake! What is to be done?

Harriet (*timidly*). You would not have encouraged me, then, if you had understood me. At least, however, I cannot be worse off than I should have been if Mr Churchill had been the person; and now—it *is* possible—for you see, that supposing—that if—strange as it may appear—But you know they were your own words, that *more* wonderful things had happened; matches of *greater* disparity had taken place than between Mr Frank Churchill and me; and, therefore, it seems as if such a thing even as this may have occurred before; and if I should be so fortunate, beyond expression, as to—if Mr Knightley should really—if *he* does not mind the disparity, I hope, dear Miss Woodhouse, you will not set yourself against it, and try and put difficulties in the way. But you are too good for that, I am sure.

Emma. Have you any idea of Mr Knightley's returning your affection?

Harriet (*modestly, but not fearfully*). Yes, I must say I have.

Emma (*aside*). Good God! is it possible—is it possible that I have been so blind even to the state of my own heart? *I* see it all now. Every moment of this day brings a fresh surprise, and every surprise is a matter of humiliation to me. How improperly have I been acting by Harriet! How inconsiderate, how irrational, how unfeeling has been my conduct! What blindness, what madness has led me on?

Harriet. Miss Woodhouse, speak to me. Why is it so much worse for me to be in love with Mr Knightley than with Mr Frank Churchill? Everyone thought *you* were in love with Mr Churchill. I thought so too, but did not like to say it.

Emma. My dear Harriet (*rousing herself*), it is the suddenness of this revelation which has bewildered me. But come, tell me all about it. What makes you so hopeful in the conviction of Mr Knightley's regard for you?

Harriet. Oh! it has been so marked. I have

been conscious of a difference in his behaviour ever since that dance. Oh! Miss Woodhouse, how nobly he behaved to me when Mr Elton *refused* to stand up with me, and he spoke so beautifully that I was not afraid of him, and when I spoke to him he listened so attentively, as if he quite enjoyed what I said.

Emma (aside). I remember he told me that on that occasion he had found her much superior to his expectation. (*Aloud.*) Well, Harriet, go on.

Harriet. From that evening, or at least from the time of your encouraging me to think of him (for though *you* meant Mr Churchill, I always meant Mr Knightley, and thought you meant him too), he has had quite a different manner towards me—a manner of kindness and sweetness. Latterly I have been more and more aware of it. When we have been all walking together, he has so often come and walked by me, and talked so very delightfully! He seemed to want to be acquainted with me.

Emma. Yes, Harriet, you are right; he has told me so himself.

Harriet. There, you see! And he has praised

me so kindly several times, I would rather not repeat what he said. But the two latest occurrences, the two of strongest promise to me—you witnessed yourself. The first was his walking with me apart from the others in the lime-walk at Donwell when he gave the strawberry party, and he took pains, I am convinced, to draw me from the rest to himself, and at first he talked to me in a more particular way than he had ever done before— in a very particular way indeed (*hanging her head*). He seemed to be almost asking me whether my affections were engaged. But as soon as you appeared likely to join us, he changed the subject, and began talking of farming. The second is his having sat talking with me here for nearly half an hour on the very last morning of his being at Hartfield — though, when he first came in, he had said that he could not stay five minutes, and he told me during our conversation that though he must go to London, it was very much against his inclinations that he left home at all.

Emma (*aside*). That is more than he acknowledged to me.

Harriet. Therefore, dear Miss Woodhouse, do you not think that I have some reason to hope? I never should have presumed to think of it at first, but for you—you told me to observe him carefully and let his behaviour be the rule of mine—and so I have.—But now I seem to feel that I may deserve him; and that if he *does* choose me, it will not be anything so very wonderful after all.

Emma (turning away to hide her bitter feelings). Harriet, I will only venture to declare that Mr Knightley is the last man in the world who would intentionally give any woman the idea of his feeling for her more than he really does.

Harriet (clasping her hands). Dear, dear Miss Woodhouse, I knew you would give me hope. You are always so good, so encouraging.

Emma (bending over her work). Harriet, look out of the window;—is not that Mr Knightley walking in the shrubbery with my father?

Harriet. It cannot be—for he was not to return for another week. (*Goes to window.*) Oh! Miss Woodhouse, you are right, it *is* Mr Knightley, and he and Mr Woodhouse are both entering the house. Oh! dear, I must go, I am too agitated to encounter him; I could not compose myself — I had better go. — May I go, Miss Woodhouse?

Emma. If you wish it, Harriet — go by all means. Good-bye.

Harriet (curtseying hurriedly). Thank you, dear Miss Woodhouse, a thousand thousand times. (*Exit.*)

Emma. Oh! God! that I had never seen her! Mr Knightley in love with Harriet Smith? Such an elevation on her side! such a debasement on his! Yet it is far, very far from impossible. Is it a new circumstance for a man of first-rate abilities to be captivated by very inferior powers? Is it new for one, perhaps too busy to seek, to be the prize of a girl who would seek him? Is it new for anything in this world to be unequal, inconsistent, or incongruous. Mr Knightley and Harriet Smith! Oh! that I had never brought her forward! — that I had left her where I ought, where he himself had once told me I ought! — Had I not, with a folly which no tongue can express, prevented her marrying the farmer, Mr Martin, who would have made her happy and respectable in a line of life to which she ought to belong—all would be well—all would be safe (*sitting to her work and bending down over it as Mr Knightley enters*).

Knightley. Emma, I have just met Harriet Smith, who told me you were alone, so I have left Mr Woodhouse comfortably by the fire in the study, and I have ventured upstairs unannounced.

Emma (*rising and giving her hand*). You are returned sooner than we hoped,—you bring good news from London?

Knightley (*sighs*). My brother and his wife are well, so are the children (*pause—he sits*).

Emma. You had a pleasant ride, I trust?

Knightley. Very——(*pause*).

Emma (*aside*). He neither looks nor speaks cheerfully. Has he communicated his plans to his brother, and been pained by their reception?

Knightley. Your father is looking well—better than when I left for London.

Emma. Yes (*a pause—she bends over her work, and he looks at her anxiously. She continues aside*). —Perhaps he wishes to speak to me of his attachment to Harriet, and is watching for encouragement to begin—but I am not equal to lead the way to such a subject—he must do it all himself — yet I cannot bear this silence,—with him, it is most unnatural. I must say *something*. (*Aloud, with a smile.*) You have some news to hear, now you are come back, that will rather surprise you.

Knightley (*quietly, and looking at her*). Have I? of what nature?

Emma. Oh! the best nature in the world—a wedding.

Knightley (*after waiting a moment as if to be sure she intended to say no more*). If you mean Miss Fairfax and Frank Churchill, I have heard that already.

Emma. Why, how is it possible? is every one in this secret?

Knightley. I had a few lines on parish business from Mr Weston this morning, and at the end he gave me a brief account of what had happened. That news was the cause of my early return.

Emma. You probably have been less surprised than any of us, for you had your suspicions. I have not forgotten that you once tried to give me caution. I wish I had attended to it—but (*with a sinking voice and a heavy sigh*) I seemed to have been doomed to blindness— (*a pause—Knightley then lays his hand on hers and takes it kindly. Emma looks at him in surprise*).

Knightley (*speaking low*). Time, my dearest Emma, time will heal the wound. Your own excellent sense; your exertions for your father's sake; I know you will not allow yourself— (*presses her hand*). I speak from feelings of the warmest friendship——indignation (*rising suddenly*). Abominable scoundrel! (*Returning and bending over the table.*) He will soon be gone. They will soon be in Yorkshire. I am sorry for *her*, for she deserves a better fate.

Emma. My dear friend, you are very kind, but you are mistaken, and I must set you right. I am not in want of that sort of compassion.

My blindness to what was going on led me to act by them in a way that I must always be ashamed of, and I was very foolishly tempted to say things of her to him which may well lay me open to unpleasant conjectures, but I have no other reason to regret that I was not in the secret earlier.

Knightley (*looking eagerly at her*). Emma, are you indeed . . .? (*Checking himself.*) No, no, I understand you—forgive me—I am pleased that you can say even so much. He is no object of regret, indeed! and it will not be very long, I hope, before that becomes the acknowledgment of more than your reason. Fortunate that your affections were not further entangled! I could never, I confess, from your manners, assure myself as to the degree of what you felt. I could only be certain that there was a preference, and a preference which I never believed him to deserve. He is a disgrace to the name of man. And is he to be rewarded with that sweet young woman? Jane, Jane, you will be a miserable creature.

Emma. Mr Knightley, I am in a very extraordinary situation. I cannot let you continue in your error; and yet, perhaps, since my manners gave such an impression, I have as much reason to be ashamed of confessing that I never have been at all attached to the person we are speaking of, as it might be natural for a woman to feel in confessing exactly the reverse. But I never have. (*A pause.*) I have very little to say for my own conduct. I was tempted by his attentions, and allowed myself to appear pleased —an old story, probably—a common case—and no more than has happened to hundreds of my sex before. Many circumstances assisted the temptation. But, let me swell out the causes ever so ingeniously, they all centre in this at last—my vanity was flattered and I allowed his attentions; but, in short, I was somehow or other safe from him.

Knightley. Hm! well, I have never had a high opinion of Frank Churchill. I can suppose, however, that I may have underrated him; my acquaintance with him has been but trifling, and even if I have not underrated him hitherto, he may yet turn out well. With such a woman he has a chance. I have no motive for wishing him ill, and for her sake, whose happiness will be involved in his good character and conduct, I shall certainly wish him well.

Emma. I have no doubt of their being happy together. I believe them to be very mutually and very sincerely attached.

Knightley (with energy). He is a most fortunate man. So early in life—at three-and-twenty—a period when, if a man chooses a wife, he generally chooses ill. At three-and-twenty to have drawn such a prize! what years of felicity that man, in all human calculation, has before him! Frank Churchill is, indeed, the favourite of fortune. He meets with a young woman at a watering-place, gains her affection, cannot even weary her by negligent treatment, and had he and all his family sought round the world for a perfect wife for him, they could not have found her superior. His aunt is in the way,—his aunt dies. He has only to speak. His friends are eager to promote his happiness. He has used everybody ill, and they are all delighted to forgive him. He is a fortunate man, indeed!

Emma. You speak as if you envied him.

Knightley. I do envy him, Emma. In one respect he is the object of my envy.

Emma (aside). He means in the right to choose where he pleases. He compares Frank Churchill to himself, Jane Fairfax to Harriet.

Knightley. You will not ask me what is the point of envy. You are determined, I see, to have no curiosity. You are wise—but *I* cannot be wise. Emma, I must tell you what you will not ask, though I may wish it unsaid the next moment.

Emma (eagerly). Oh! then, don't speak it, don't speak it—take a little time, consider, do not commit yourself.

Knightley (stiffly). Thank you.

Emma (aside). Oh, I have given him pain! He is wishing to confide in me, to consult me; perhaps I might assist his resolution, or reconcile him to it.

Knightley. I fear I must be going now; goodbye. (*Puts out his hand as he rises.*)

Emma (detaining it). No—do not go—I stopped you ungraciously just now, Mr Knightley, and, I am afraid, gave you pain. But if you have any wish to speak openly to me as a friend, or to ask my opinion of anything that you may have in contemplation—as a friend, indeed, you may command me. I will hear whatever you like. I will tell you exactly what I think.

Knightley. As a friend! Emma, that I fear is a word—No, I have no wish. Stay, yes, why should I hesitate? I have gone too far already for concealment. Emma, I accept your offer, extraordinary as it may seem, I accept it, and refer myself to you as a friend (*looking earnestly into her eyes*). Tell me, then, have I no chance of ever succeeding?

Emma (overcome). Good Heaven!

Knightley. My dearest Emma, for dearest you will always be, whatever the event of this hour's conversation, my dearest, most beloved Emma—tell me at once. Say "No" if it is to be said. You are silent (*with animation*) absolutely silent! at present I ask no more.

(*Emma sinks into a chair, covering up her face with her hands.*)

Knightley. I cannot make speeches, Emma. If I loved you less, I might be able to talk about it more. But you know what I am. You hear nothing but truth from me. I have blamed you and lectured you, and you have borne it as no other woman in England would have borne it. Bear with the truths I would tell you now, dearest Emma, as well as you have borne with them. God knows, I have been a very indifferent lover. Look up, Emma, my dearest, look at me—(*she does so*). Say that you understand me.—Say you understand my feelings—and will return them if you can. At present I ask only to hear, once to hear your voice.

Emma (*faintly*). Mr Knightley, what can I say? How can I say it? When you first spoke, believe me, I had no idea, no thought of what you wished to say. How inconsistent must my conduct have appeared in refusing to hear you one moment, and soliciting your confidence the next—yet could I have dared to hope that you would speak to me as you have done, I should through very shame have silenced you for ever.

Knightley. My dearest, best beloved Emma! I too had little thought when first I entered here to try my influence. Jealousy of Frank Churchill drove me from the country. I went to London to learn to be indifferent; but I had gone to the wrong place. There was too much domestic happiness in my brother's house; but I stayed on, however, vigorously, day after day, till this very morning's post conveyed the history of Jane Fairfax. Then, with the gladness which must be felt, nay, which I did not scruple to feel, was there so much fond solicitude, so much keen anxiety for you, that I could stay no longer. I rode home at once and walked up here to see how this sweetest and best of all creatures, faultless in spite of all her faults, bore the discovery. I found you agitated and low; Frank Churchill was a villain. I heard you declare that you had never loved him. Frank Churchill's character was not so desperate; and now, tell me that you are my own Emma by hand and word.

Emma (*putting her hands in his*). Mr Knightley, I am your own Emma, by word and hand.

Knightley (*bending over Emma's hands*). "Mr Knightley," you always called me "Mr Knightley," and from habit it has not so very formal a sound, and yet it is formal. I want you to call me something else, but I do not know what.

Emma. I remember once calling you "George" in one of my amiable fits, about ten years' ago. I did it because I thought it might offend you; but, as you made no objection, I never did it again.

Knightley. And cannot you call me "George" now?

Emma. Impossible? I never can call you anything but "Mr Knightley." I will not promise even to equal the elegant terseness of Mrs Elton by calling you Mr K—. But I will promise to call you once by your Christian name. I do not say when, but perhaps you may guess where; — in the building in which N. takes M. for better, for worse.

Knightley (*with emotion*). My Emma.

[*Exeunt.*

End of Scene.

THE PROPOSAL OF MR COLLINS.

Mrs Bennet, Elizabeth Bennet, Mr Collins.

From " Pride and Prejudice."

Costumes.

Mr Collins in black, with a high choker and cravat tied in front.

Elizabeth. Pale primrose dress, the lappels of the bodice and the hem of the skirt embroidered in gold and white; clear muslin chemisette, rucked under-sleeves of the same.

Elizabeth Bennet and Mr Collins.

THE PROPOSAL OF MR COLLINS.

Characters.

Mrs Bennet, Elizabeth Bennet, Mr Collins.

N.B. — "*Her* (*Mrs Bennet*) mind was less difficult to develope. She was a woman of mean understanding, little information, and uncertain temper. When she was discontented, she fancied herself nervous. The business of her life was to get her daughters married; its solace was visiting and news."—*Pride and Prejudice*, Chap I.

"The greatest part of his (*Mr Collins*) life had been spent under the guidance of an illiterate and miserly father. . . . The subjection in which his father had brought him up had given him originally great humility of manner, but it was now a good deal counteracted by the self-conceit of a weak head, living in retirement, and the consequential feeling of early and unexpected prosperity. . . . Having now a good home and a very sufficient income, he intended to marry; and in seeking a reconciliation with the Longbourn family (*The Bennets*) he had a wife in view, as he meant to choose one of the daughters, if he found them as handsome and amiable as they were represented by common report. This was his plan of amends—of atonement—for inheriting their father's estate, and he thought it an excellent one, full of eligibility and suitableness, and excessively generous and disinterested on his own part."—*Pride and Prejudice*, Chap. XV., Vol. I.

" The situation of your mother's family, though objectionable, was nothing in comparison of that total want of propriety so frequently, so almost uniformly betrayed by herself, by your three younger sisters, and occasionally even by your father,—

pardon me—it pains me to offend you. But amidst your concern for the defects of your nearest relations, and your displeasure at this representation of them, let it give you consolation to consider, that to have conducted yourselves so as to avoid any share of the like censure, is praise no less generally bestowed on you and your eldest sister, than it is honourable to the sense and disposition of both."—*Quotation from Darcy's letter to Elizabeth Bennet,* Vol. II., Chapter XXXV.

Scene.—The morning-room at Longbourne.

Properties required: There is a good-sized table L. Chairs, sofas, and other tables about the room. The furniture is good, but a little shabby and vulgar, and formal. Door R. enter Elizabeth with household needlework. She walks to the table.

Elizabeth. Well! if my father was hopeful of finding our cousin, Mr Collins, far from sensible, I cannot think he is disappointed, for the deficiencies of nature have been but little assisted by education, and though he has belonged to one of the Universities, he evidently merely kept the necessary terms without forming there any useful acquaintance.

Enter Mrs Bennet (going to her work). Well, Lizzie, what do you think of your cousin, Mr Collins. I am sure he is a very fine young man, in spite of his being next in the entail—though, to be sure, I cannot bear to hear that mentioned—and I do think it is the hardest thing in the world that your father's estate should be entailed away from his own children, and I am sure, if I had been him, I should have tried long ago to do something about it.

Elizabeth. My dear ma'am, let me try and explain again the nature of an entail.

Mrs Bennet. Not one word, Eliza. It is trying enough to my nerves to know that we must submit to such a thing simply because of Mr Bennet's indifference to what becomes of us all when he is dead, without having it all explained to me. However, I don't suppose Mr Collins can help it, and as he has seemed, since the very first day we saw him, a week ago, willing to make amends by one or other of you girls, I am not the person to discourage him.

Elizabeth. Certainly not, my dear ma'am.

Mrs Bennet. Not but what at first I thought he wanted your sister Jane. It was quite right and proper, considering she was the eldest and by far the best-looking of you all. But when I found that he was thinking of her, I gave him a hint that she was not to be had for the asking. I don't want to spoil Jane's chance with Bingley, and so I just put it right, you know.

Elizabeth. I have no doubt you acted wisely, ma'am.

Mrs Bennet. Well, Lizzie, I did for the best. When he told me his plans, and that he had come to Longbourne to choose a wife among you, I said, "Mr Collins, I cannot but be very gratified by your confidence, and as to my younger daughters, I cannot take upon myself to say—I could not positively answer," for I did not want to appear *too* pleased with his attentions "and I do not know of any prepossessions, but my *eldest* daughter, I must just mention—I feel it incumbent on me to hint—is likely to be very soon engaged,"—and it is marvellous how soon he abandoned all idea of Jane. But hush, here he comes. (*Enter Mr Collins*).

Mr Collins. May I hope, madam, for your interest with your fair daughter Elizabeth, when I solicit for the honour of a private audience with her in the course of the morning.

Mrs Bennet (*starting up*). Oh! dear! yes—certainly. I am sure Lizzie will be very happy. I am sure she can have no objection. (*Going.*)

Elizabeth. Dear ma'am, do not go. I beg you will not go. Mr Collins must excuse me. He can have nothing to say to me that anybody need not hear. I am going away myself. (*Also going.*)

Mrs Bennet. No, no, nonsense, Lizzie. I desire you will stay where you are (*seeing that Elizabeth is determined to go*). Lizzie, I *insist* upon your staying, and hearing Mr Collins. (*Exit.*)

Elizabeth (*aside*). Well! if it has to be—I may as well get it over as soon and as quietly as possible.

Mr Collins. Believe me, my dear Miss Elizabeth, that your modesty, so far from doing you any disservice, rather adds to your other perfections. You would have been less amiable in my eyes had there *not* been this little unwillingness; but allow me to assure you, that I have your respected mother's permission for this address. You can hardly doubt the purport of my discourse, however your natural delicacy may lead you to dissemble; my attentions have been too marked to be mistaken. Almost as soon as I entered the house, I singled you out as the companion of my future life. But, before I am run away with by my feelings on this subject, perhaps it would be advisable for me to state my reasons for marrying—and, moreover, for coming into Hertfordshire with the design of selecting a wife—as I certainly did.

Elizabeth (aside). The idea of this man being run away with by his feelings.

Mr Collins. My reasons for marrying are—first, that I think it a right thing for every clergyman in easy circumstances (like myself) to set the example of matrimony in his parish; secondly, I am convinced it will add very greatly to my happiness; and thirdly—which perhaps I ought to have mentioned earlier, that it is the particular advice and recommendation of the very noble lady whom I have the honour of calling patroness. Twice has she condescended to give me her opinion (unasked, too!) on this subject; and it was but the very Saturday night before I left Hunsford, between our pools at quadrille, that she said, " Mr Collins, you must marry—a clergyman like you must marry. Choose properly, choose a gentlewoman for *my* sake; and for your *own*, let her be an active, useful sort of person not brought up high, but able to make a small income go a good way. This is my advice. Find such a woman as soon as you can, bring her to Hunsford, and I will visit her." Allow me, by the way, to observe, my fair cousin, that I do not reckon the notice and kindness of Lady de Burgh as among the least of the advantages in my power to offer. You will find her manners beyond anything I can describe, and your wit and vivacity, I think, must be acceptable to her, especially when tempered with the silence and respect which her rank will inevitably excite.

Elizabeth (*aside*). How am I to stop the man?

Mr Collins. This much for my general intention in favour of matrimony; it remains to be told why my views were directed to Longbourn instead of my own neighbourhood, where I assure you there are many amiable young women. But the fact is, that being, as I am, to inherit this estate after the death of your honoured father (*reverentially*) (who, however, may live many years longer) I could not satisfy myself without resolving to choose a wife from among his daughters, that the loss to them might be as little as possible when the melancholy event takes place, which, however, as I have already said, may not be for several years. This has been my motive, my fair cousin, and I flatter myself it will not sink me in your esteem. And now, nothing remains for me but to assure you, in the most animated language, of the violence of my affection. To fortune I am perfectly indifferent, and shall make no demand of that nature on your father, since I am well aware that it could not be complied with, and that one thousand pounds in the 4 per cents., which will not be yours till after your mother's decease, is all that you may ever be entitled to. On that head I shall, therefore, be uniformly silent; and you may assure yourself that no ungenerous reproach shall ever pass my lips when we are married.

Elizabeth. You are too hasty sir; you forget that I have made no answer. Let me do it without further loss of time. Accept my thanks for the compliment you are paying me. I am very sensible of the honour of your proposals, but it is impossible for me to do otherwise than decline them.

Collins (*waving his hand*). I am not now to learn that it is usual with young ladies to reject the addresses of the man whom they secretly mean to accept, when he first applies for their favour; and that sometimes the refusal is repeated a second or even a third time. I am, therefore, by no means discouraged by what you have just said, and shall hope to lead you to the altar ere long.

Elizabeth. Upon my word, sir, your hope is rather an extraordinary one after my declaration. I do assure you that I am not one of those young ladies (if such young ladies there are) who are so daring as to risk their happiness on the chance of being asked a second time. I am perfectly serious in my refusal; you could not make me happy, and I am convinced that I am the last woman in the world who could make you so. Nay, were your friend, Lady Catherine, to know me, I am persuaded she would find me in every respect ill qualified for the situation.

Collins (gravely). Were it certain that Lady Catherine would think so—but I cannot imagine that her ladyship would at all disapprove of you. And, you may be certain that when I have the honour of seeing her again, I shall speak in the highest terms of your modesty, economy, and other amiable qualifications.

Elizabeth. Indeed, Mr Collins, all praise of me will be unnecessary; you must give me leave to judge for myself, and pay me the compliment of believing what I say: I wish you very happy and very rich, and by refusing your hand, do all in my power to prevent your being otherwise. In making me the offer, you must have satisfied the delicacy of your feelings with regard to my family, and may take possession of Longbourn estate whenever it falls without any self-reproach (*rising*). This matter may be considered, therefore, as finally settled.

Mr Collins. When I do myself the honour of speaking to you next on the subject, I shall hope to receive a more favourable answer than you have now given me; though I am far from accusing you of cruelty at present, because I know it to be an established custom of your sex to reject a man on the *first* application, and perhaps you have even now said as much to encourage my suit as would be consistent with the true delicacy of the female character.

Elizabeth (warmly). Really, Mr Collins, you puzzle me exceedingly. If what I have hitherto said can appear to you in the form of encouragement, I know not how to express my refusal in such a way as may convince you of its being one.

Collins (smiling). You must give me leave to flatter myself, my dear cousin, that your refusal of my addresses is merely words of course. My reasons for believing it are briefly these— It does not appear to me that my hand is unworthy your acceptance, or that the establishment I can offer would be other than highly desirable. My situation in life, my connections with the family of De Burgh, and my relationship to your own, are circumstances highly in my favour; and you should take it into further consideration, that in spite of your manifold attractions, it is by no means certain that another offer of marriage may ever be made you—your portion is unhappily so small, that it will in all likelihood undo the effects of your loveliness and amiable qualifications. As I must therefore conclude that you are not serious in your rejection of me, I shall choose to attribute it to your wish of increasing my love by suspense, according to the usual practice of elegant females.

Elizabeth. I do assure you, sir, that I have no pretension whatever of that kind of elegance which consists in tormenting a respectable man. I would rather be paid the compliment of being believed sincere. I thank you again and again for the honour you have done me in your proposals, but to accept them is absolutely impossible. My feelings in every respect forbid it. Can I speak plainer? Do not consider me now as an elegant female, intending to plague you, but as a rational creature, speaking the truth from her heart.

Collins (*with awkward gallantry*). You are uniformly charming! and I am persuaded that when sanctioned by the express authority of both your excellent parents, my proposals will not fail of being acceptable.

Elizabeth. To such perseverance in wilful

THE PROPOSAL OF MR COLLINS. 117

self-deception I can make no reply; but if you persist in considering my repeated refusals as flattering encouragement, I shall apply to my father, whose negative will no doubt be uttered in such a manner as must be decisive, and whose behaviour at least will not be mistaken for the affectation and coquetry of an "elegant female." (*Enter Mrs Bennet.*)

Mrs Bennet. Well, Mr Collins, allow me to congratulate you—and myself.

Mr Collins (*smiling complacently*). I trust I have every reason to be satisfied with the result of our interview, since the refusal with which my fair cousin has replied to my proposals comes naturally from her bashful modesty and the delicacy of her character.

Mrs Bennet. Her refusal? Why, Lizzie, what is the meaning of this—do you refuse Mr Collins?

Elizabeth. I do indeed, ma'am.

Mrs Bennet. Oh! Mr Collins, do not pay any attention to her. Depend upon it, she shall be brought to reason. I will speak to her about it myself privately. She is a very headstrong, foolish girl, and does not know her own interest; but I will *make* her know it.

Mr Collins (*gravely*). Pardon me for interrupting you, madam. But if she is really headstrong and foolish, I know not whether she would altogether be a very desirable wife to a man in my situation, who naturally looks for happiness in the marriage state. If, therefore, Miss Elizabeth actually persists in rejecting my suit, perhaps it were better not to force her into accepting me, because if liable to such defects of temper, she could not contribute much to my felicity.

Elizabeth (*interrupting*). That is very true, Mr Collins.

Mrs Bennet. Sir, you quite misunderstand me. Lizzie is only headstrong in such matters as these. In everything else she is as good-natured a girl as ever lived. Yes, you are, Lizzie, and I insist on you accepting Mr Collins.

Elizabeth. Ma'am, ma'am. I cannot, I do not care for him.

Mrs Bennet. Now, I do insist upon it, Lizzie,

that you hold your tongue and let Mr Collins and me have a little conversation together.

Mr Collins (*stiffly*). My dear madam, let us be for ever silent on this point. Far be it from me to resent the behaviour of your daughter. Resignation to inevitable evil is the duty of us all. You will not, I hope, consider me as showing any disrespect to your family by now withdrawing all pretensions to your daughter's favour. My conduct may, I fear, be objectionable in accepting my dismission from *her* lips instead of your own. But we are all liable to error—I have certainly meant well through the whole affair. My object has been to secure an amiable companion for myself, with due consideration for the advantage of all your family, and if my *manner* has been at all reprehensible, I beg here to apologise. (*Exit, with a bow.*)

Mrs Bennet (*calling after him*). Oh! Mr Collins—(*turning angrily to Elizabeth*), and there you stand, looking as unconcerned as may be, and caring no more for us all than if you were at York—provided you can have your own way. But I will tell you what, Miss Lizzie, if you take it into your head to go on refusing every offer of marriage in this way, you will never get a husband at all; and I am sure I do not know who is to maintain you when your father is dead—*I* shall not be able to keep you, and so I warn you. I have done with you from this very day—I shall never speak to you again, and you will find me as good as my word—I have no pleasure in talking to undutiful children. Not that I have much pleasure, indeed, in talking to anybody. People who suffer as I do from nervous complaints can have no great inclination for talking. Nobody can tell what I suffer! but it is always so, those who do not complain are never pitied—and it is all owing to you—to your wilfulness and bad temper.

Elizabeth (*coaxingly*). Ah, ma'am, do not be hard on me. Think of my sister Jane. How lovely she is. How much admired. How willing *she* will be to listen to Mr Bingley. Let us go and tell her about it all. She will agree with us both.

Mrs Bennet (softened). Well, Lizzie, I suppose I must be content with *one* sensible girl among you all, but I should be thankful to have *you* off my hands.

(*Exeunt Mrs Bennet and Elizabeth.*)

End of Scene.

LADY CATHERINE'S VISIT.

From " Pride and Prejudice," Vol. I., Chap XXIX.

Costumes.

Lady Catherine. Large hat trimmed with white feathers, and violet silk handkerchief, worn over a ruched cap. Dress of cinnamon brown satin; the bodice cut V-shaped in front; a high ruche of white muslin round the neck; open front of bodice being frilled with white lace. Pelisse of deep violet cloth. Silver-headed black stick; long-handled eyeglass.

Elizabeth. Dress of white Indian muslin—the bodice made high in front and gathered in the centre of the bosom into a long gold brooch. A Spencer waist trimmed round back and down the sides with a frill of the muslin, sleeves tied with pale green ribbon. Pale green ribbon girdle.

Lady Catherine and Elizabeth Bennet.

LADY CATHERINE'S VISIT.

Characters.

Lady Catherine de Burgh, Elizabeth Bennet.

N.B.—" Elizabeth's courage did not fail her. She had heard nothing of Lady Catherine that spoke her awful from any extraordinary talents or miraculous virtue, and the mere stateliness of money and rank she thought she could witness without trepidation. . . . Her air was not conciliating, nor was her manner of receiving them . . . such as to make her visitors forget their inferior rank. She was not rendered formidable by silence; but whatever she said was spoken in so authoritative a tone as marked her self-importance . . . delivering her opinion on every subject in so decisive a manner as proved that she was not used to have her judgment controverted."—*Pride and Prejudice*, Vol I., Chap. XXIX.

"There was a mixture of sweetness and archness in her (*Elizabeth's*) manner which made it difficult for her to affront anybody, and Darcy had never been so bewitched by any woman as he was by her."—Vol. I., Chap. X.

(*Elizabeth.*) "There is a stubbornness about me that never can bear to be frightened at the will of others. My courage always rises with every attempt to intimidate me."—*Pride and Prejudice*, Vol. I., Chap. XXXI.

Scene—The morning-room at Longbourn. The furniture is comfortable, but a little shabby; it also wears a faded look of gaudiness, and is arranged in a stiff and formal manner.

Properties required:—If possible a long French window at the back for Lady Catherine to enter. If not practicable a door to the L.

with a screen in front of it, behind which the window must be imagined. Door R.

Elizabeth. So all is settled peaceably and amicably in this turbulent family of ours. Dear Jane has attained her wish at last, and is engaged to Mr Bingley, and Lydia is married. Lydia, who caused us so much unspeakable misery but a few weeks back, by eloping with Mr Wickham, is married, and the Bennets are now acknowledged to be the luckiest family in the world, though only a little while before we were generally proved to be marked out by misfortune.

How quickly and easily all this has been arranged, and by whom? By Mr Darcy, whose character I once so misjudged, whose proposal of marriage I treated with such scorn, but whom now my heart tells me I sincerely love and esteem. To-morrow he is to come to see us with Bingley. Bingley will have eyes for none but Jane. Will Mr Darcy be satisfied to spend the time with me, or will he have too keen a remembrance of my refusal when he was staying with Lady Catherine at Rosings? Good heaven! were she to know what passed between us, what would her feelings be.

Going to the window. I thought I heard the sound of a carriage. Who can it be? It is too early for visitors, and, besides, I know neither the servant nor the livery. The horses are post, too. Good Heaven! it is Lady Catherine de Burgh. What can she want here? She has seen me, and evidently means to come in through the window. (*Enter Lady Catherine de Burgh, C. through the French window or from behind the screen. She bows stiffly to Elizabeth, who curtseys.*)

Lady C. (*sitting*). I hope you are well, Miss Bennet.

Elizabeth. Thank you, very well. Allow me to call my mother.

Lady C. No, I thank you. It is you I have come all this way to see.

Elizabeth (*surprised*). I am greatly honoured.

Lady C. You have a very small park here.

Elizabeth (smiling). It is certainly not to compare with Rosings, but, I assure you, it is quite large enough for our use.

Lady C. (snifs). This must be a most inconvenient sitting-room for the evening in summer; the windows are full west.

Elizabeth. We only sit here in the morning. (*Aside.*) Heaven! how could I think her like her nephew.

Lady C. You can be at no loss, Miss Bennet, to understand the reason of my journey hither. Your own heart, your own conscience must tell you why I come.

Elizabeth (with unaffected astonishment). Indeed, you are mistaken, madam, I have not been at all able to account for the honour of seeing you here.

Lady C. (angrily). Miss Bennet, you ought to know I am not to be trifled with. But, however insincere *you* may choose to be, you shall not find *me* so. My character has ever been celebrated for its sincerity and frankness, and in a cause of such moment as this I shall certainly not depart from it. A report of a most alarming nature reached me two days ago. I was told that not only your elder sister was on the point of being most advantageously married, but that *you*, that Miss Elizabeth Bennet, would, in all likelihood, be soon afterwards united to my nephew — my own nephew — Mr Darcy. Though I *knew* it must be a scandalous falsehood — though I would not injure him so much as to suppose the truth of it possible, I instantly resolved on setting off for this place, that I might make my sentiments known to you.

Elizabeth (surprised and angry). If you believed it impossible to be true, I wonder you took the trouble of coming so far. What could your ladyship propose by it?

Lady C. At once to insist upon having such a report universally contradicted.

Elizabeth (coolly). Your coming to Longbourn to see me will be rather a confirmation of it; if, indeed, such a report is in existence.

Lady C. If! do you then pretend to be ignorant of it? Has it not been industriously circulated by yourselves. Do you not know that such a report is spread abroad?

Elizabeth. I never heard that it was.

Lady C. And can you likewise declare that there is no *foundation* for it?

Elizabeth. I do not pretend to possess equal frankness with your ladyship. *You* may ask questions, which *I* shall not choose to answer.

Lady C. This is not to be borne! Miss Bennet, I insist on being satisfied. Has he, has my nephew, made you an offer of marriage?

Elizabeth. Your ladyship has declared it to be impossible.

Lady C. It ought to be so; it must be so, while he retains the use of his reason. But your arts and allurements may, in a moment of infatuation, have made him forget what he owes to himself and to all his family. You may have drawn him in.

Elizabeth. If I have, I shall be the last person to confess it.

Lady C. Miss Bennet, do you know who I am? I have not been accustomed to such language as this. I am almost the nearest relation he has in the world, and am entitled to know all his dearest concerns.

Elizabeth. But you are not entitled to know *mine;* nor will such behaviour as this ever induce me to be explicit.

Lady C. Let me be rightly understood. This match, to which you have the presumption to aspire, can never take place. No, never; Mr Darcy is engaged to *my daughter.* Now what have you to say.

Elizabeth (*quietly*). Only this, that if it is so, you can have no reason to suppose he will make an offer to me.

Lady C. The engagement between them is of a peculiar kind. From their infancy they have been intended for each other. It was the favourite wish of *his* mother as well as of hers. While in their cradles, we planned the union, and now, at the moment when the wishes of both sisters would be accomplished, is their marriage to be prevented by a young woman of inferior birth, of no importance in the world, and wholly unallied to the family! Do you pay no regard to the wishes of his friends—to his tacit engagement with Miss de Burgh? Are you lost to every feeling of propriety and delicacy? Have you not heard me say that from his earliest hours he was destined for his cousin?

Elizabeth. Yes! and I had heard it before. But what is that to me? If there is no other objection to my marrying your nephew, I shall certainly not be kept from it by knowing that his mother and aunt wished him to marry Miss de Burgh. You both did as much as you could, in planning the marriage; its completion depended on others. If Mr Darcy is neither by honour nor inclination confined to his cousin, why is not he to make another choice? And if I am that choice, why may not I accept him?

Lady C. Because honour, decorum, prudence —nay, *interest*, forbid it. Yes, Miss Bennet, interest; for do not expect to be noticed by any of his family or friends if you wilfully act against the inclinations of all. You will be censured, slighted, and despised by everyone connected with him. Your alliance will be a disgrace; your name will never be mentioned by any of us.

Elizabeth. These are heavy misfortunes indeed. But the wife of Mr Darcy must have such extraordinary sources of happiness necessarily attached to her situation that she could, upon the whole, have no cause to repine.

Lady C. Obstinate, headstrong girl! I am ashamed of you!—But you are to understand me, Miss Bennet; I came here with the determined resolution of carrying my purpose, nor will I be dissuaded from it. I have not been used to submit to any person's whims. I have not been in the habit of brooking disappointment.

Elizabeth. *That* will make your ladyship's situation at present more pitiable, but it will have no effect on *me*.

Lady C. I will not be interrupted! Hear me in silence. My daughter and my nephew are formed for each other. They are descended, on the maternal side, from the same noble line; and on the father's, from respectable, honourable, and ancient, though untitled families.

Their fortune on both sides is splendid. They are destined for each other by the voice of every member of their respective houses; and what is to divide them? — the upstart pretensions of a young woman without family, connections, or fortune! Is this to be endured? But it must not, shall not be! If you were sensible of your own good, you would not wish to quit the sphere in which you have been brought up.

Elizabeth. In marrying your nephew, I should not consider myself as quitting that sphere. He is a gentleman; I am a gentleman's daughter: so far we are equal.

Lady C. True, you are a gentleman's daughter; but who was your mother? Who are your uncles and aunts? Do not imagine me ignorant of their condition.

Elizabeth. Whatever my connections may be, if your nephew does not object to them, they can be nothing to you.

Lady C. Tell me, once for all, are you engaged to him?

Elizabeth (after slight deliberation). I am not.

Lady C. (pleased). Ah! and will you promise me never to enter into such an engagement?

Elizabeth. I will make no promise of the kind.

Lady C. Miss Bennet, I am shocked and astonished. I expected to find a more reasonable young woman. But do not deceive yourself into a belief that I will ever recede. I shall not go away till you have given me the assurance I require.

Elizabeth. And I certainly *never* shall give it. I am not to be intimidated into anything so wholly unreasonable. Your ladyship wants Mr Darcy to marry your daughter; but would my giving you your wished-for promise make *their* marriage at all more probable? supposing him to be attached to me, would *my* refusing to accept his hand make him wish to bestow it on his cousin? Allow me to say, Lady Catherine, that the arguments with which you have supported this extraordinary application have been as frivolous as the application was ill-judged. You have widely mistaken my character if you think I can be worked on by such persuasions as these. How far your nephew might approve of your interference in *his* affairs I cannot tell, but you have certainly no right to concern yourself in mine. I must beg, therefore, to be importuned no further on the subject.

Lady C. Not so hasty, if you please. I have by no means done. To all the objections I have already urged, I have still another to add. I am no stranger to the particulars of your youngest sister's infamous elopement. I know it all; that the young man's marrying her was a patched-up business—at the expense of your father and uncle. And is such a girl to be my nephew's sister? Heaven and earth!—of what are you thinking?

Elizabeth (rising angrily). You can now have nothing further to say. You have insulted me in every possible method. I must beg to be allowed to leave you. (*Curtseys.*)

Lady C. (rising, highly incensed). Stay, Miss Bennet. You have no regard then for the honour and credit of my nephew! Unfeeling, selfish girl! do you not consider that a connection with you must disgrace him in the eyes of everybody.

Elizabeth. Lady Catherine, I have nothing further to say—you know my sentiments.

Lady C. You are then resolved to have him?

Elizabeth. I have said no such thing. I am only resolved to act in that manner which will, in my own opinion, constitute my happiness, without reference to *you*, or to any person so wholly unconnected with me.

Lady C. It is well! You refuse then to oblige me. You refuse to obey the claims of duty, honour, and gratitude. You are determined to ruin him in the opinion of all his friends, and make him the contempt of the world.

Elizabeth. Neither duty, nor honour, nor gratitude, has any possible claim on me in the present instance. No principle of either would be violated by my marriage with Mr Darcy. And with regard to the resentment of his family or the indignation of the world, if the former *were* excited by his marrying me, it would not give me one moment's concern—and the world in general would have too much sense to join in the scorn.

Lady C. And this is your real opinion! This is your final resolve! Very well, I shall now know how to act. Do not imagine, Miss Bennet, that your ambition will ever be gratified. I came to try you. I hoped to find you reasonable; but depend upon it, I will carry my point.

Elizabeth. Good-day to you, Lady Catherine.

Lady C. (*at the window or screen*). I take no leave of you, Miss Bennet. I send no compliments to your mother. You deserve no such attention. I am most seriously displeased. (*Exit Lady Catherine.*)

Elizabeth. I could tell her truthfully I am *not* engaged to Mr Darcy, but she little guessed the rest. Yet I do not think he can be quite indifferent to me, or surely she would not have taken the trouble—If he comes to-morrow with Bingley, as he arranged, I shall dare to hope (*sighs happily*). Perhaps I, too, may learn to think the Bennet family lucky in spite of Lady Catherine de Burgh.

[Exit.

End of Scene.